IDEAS FOR GREAT
BATHROOMS

By the Editors of Sunset and Southern Living

A sunken whirlpool tub provides both focus and function. For a closer look at this bathroom, see pages 30–31.

This deck-mounted spout not only looks great, but fills a tub quickly, too. For details on tubs and fittings, see pages 74–76.

Book Editor
Scott Atkinson

Coordinating Editor
Suzanne Normand Mathison

Contributing Editor
Carolyn C. Adams

Design
Joe di Chiarro

Illustrations
Mark Pechenik

Photo Stylist
JoAnn Masaoka Van Atta

Photographers: Mark Citret, 63 top right; **Philip Harvey,** 1, 2, 4 left and middle, 5 left and right, 6, 22, 24, 25, 26, 27, 30, 31, 36, 37, 38, 39, 40, 41, 42, 43, 44, 45, 46, 47, 48, 49, 50, 51, 56, 57, 58, 59, 60, 63 bottom, 65 top left and bottom right, 66 top and middle, 68, 69, 70 bottom right, 72, 74, 75 top, 76, 77 middle left, middle right, and bottom, 78 top left and bottom right, 79 top, 80 left, 81, 83 top right, 85, 86 top, 87, 88, 90, 92; **Stephen Marley,** 67 top, 89; **Jack McDowell,** 83 middle left; **Norman A. Plate,** 21 bottom, 70 top; **Marvin Sloben,** 21 top; **Smallbone, Inc.,** 63 top left; **Darrow M. Watt,** 82 top right; **Alan Weintraub,** 4 right, 34, 35, 52, 53, 54, 55, 73 left, 75 bottom, 77 top left, 84, 93; **Tom Wyatt,** 5 middle, 28, 29, 32, 33, 64, 65 top right, 66 bottom, 67 middle right and bottom left, 70 middle left and bottom left, 71, 73 right, 78 bottom left, 79 bottom right, 80 right, 82 bottom left, 83 bottom right, 86 bottom.

More Than Just Bathrooms . . .

The bathroom, once ignored or maligned, is now the scene of a real design renaissance. New styles, new materials, and multiuse floor plans are transforming the bath into a haven of both efficiency and comfort.

Plot the bath of your dreams with this book as your guide. You'll find the latest in both gleaming fixtures and efficient designs. From a cozy armchair, you can examine case studies—18 up-to-the-minute bath designs in full color. Or bone up on European cabinets, whirlpool tubs, ultra-low-flush toilets, and halogen downlights. If you're ready to dig in, you'll also find a solid introduction to bathroom planning.

Many bath professionals and homeowners provided information and encouragement or allowed us to look at their new creations. We'd especially like to thank the National Kitchen & Bath Association; The Bath & Beyond; BK Design Center; Casella Lighting Co.; Dillon Tile Supply, Inc.; Import Tile Co., Inc.; Menlo Park Hardware Co.; and Tileshop. We'd also like to acknowledge The American Cancer Society Decorator Showcase and the San Francisco Decorator Showcase.

Special thanks go to Marcia Morrill Williamson for carefully editing the manuscript.

Cover: Colorful ceramic tiles—laid in a festival of shapes and patterns—helped transform this master bath space. For additional details on this remodel, see pages 34–35. Bathroom designed by Mark Rebarchik and Brett Heller. Cover design by Susan Bryant. Photography by Alan Weintraub. Photo styling by JoAnn Masaoka Van Atta.

Editor: Elizabeth L. Hogan

Second printing June 1992

CONTENTS

MAKE A BIG SPLASH

The news is out: people want bathrooms to be bold, beautiful, and—especially—comfortable.

It wasn't always that way. The first wooden bathtubs, scenes of the painfully elaborate Saturday night scrubs immortalized by Western movies, appeared in the mid 1800s. Soon these leaky vessels were replaced by cast-iron tubs—essentially horse troughs with legs. The bathroom as we know it came indoors only in the 1920s, and with no great fanfare. Health and privacy concerns, not aesthetics, prompted the move.

A new but mandatory 5- by 7-foot space—a "terra incognita"—now appeared on architects' and tract builders' plans.

Today, whether due to the development of two-earner families, or simply to the whims of the "me" generation, homeowners are requiring their architects and designers to give new thought to the use of this space. The bathroom is no longer an "out-of-sight, out-of-mind" proposition; it's a rewarding part of the good life.

The new bathrooms tend to be bigger. They tend to be compartmentalized for multiple uses. And many are geared for relaxation as well as efficiency. The whirlpool tub—a trimmed-down version of the outdoor spa—has become a focal point for many designs. The "master suite"—a formal integration of bedroom, bath, and auxiliary spaces—is perhaps the crowning expression of the bathroom's new-found identity. Exercise rooms, saunas, steam showers, grooming alcoves, walk-in dressing wings, even indoor atriums are all new master-suite options.

DESIGNER: OSBURN DESIGN

Decorative strip lighting

DESIGNER: RICK SAMBOL/KITCHEN CONSULTANTS

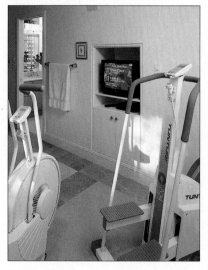

Exercise room

ARCHITECT: CARSON BOWLER/BOWLER & COOK ARCHITECTS

Pedestal sink

As with contemporary kitchen design, there's a freer mixing of materials and styles; an emphasis on artificial lighting and an appreciation of natural light expressed in the use of windows, skylights, and glass block; an interest in raised ceilings and soffit details; and a new creativity in approaches to cabinetry.

Antique fixtures and fittings are being treated with fresh respect, but they're teamed with a huge assortment of new styles and finishes.

There's a new attention to water conservation. Manufacturers are offering ultra-low-flush toilets, low-flow shower heads, and sink faucets that save water or shut off when the user's hand is withdrawn.

Safety is a concern. It's now much easier to find sturdy grab bars, nonskid fixtures, and shatterproof materials. You can buy pressure-balancing or temperature-limiting plumbing fittings to prevent scalds.

As the population ages and we gain new awareness of the needs of the physically challenged, the barrier-free bath is receiving deserved attention. Besides easy access, a major goal for today's barrier-free bath is aesthetic: it shouldn't *look* like a barrier-free bath.

Brainstorming a new bathroom is a threefold process: planning the space, defining a style, and choosing components. That's the sequence this book follows. You can tackle these steps in order or browse freely, using the book as a detailed planning resource or simply choosing images and ideas to help your architect or designer understand more clearly what you want.

Ready to begin transforming that old bath? Simply turn the page.

Modular fixture handles

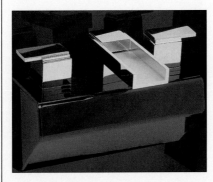

Spread-fit faucet

ARCHITECT: REMICK ASSOCIATES

Heated towel bar

A PLANNING PRIMER

What look do you like? Warm and traditional, high-tech, or colorfully whimsical? The styles may be different, but successful baths have a lot in common. When a bathroom looks great and functions well, you can be sure that hours of planning went into its realization. Behind those shiny new fixtures and tiles are codes and clearances, critical dimensions, and effective design principles.

Use this chapter as a workbook for basic planning. We help you evaluate your existing bathroom first. Then we guide you through layout and design basics, and finish up by explaining how design and construction professionals can help you.

For inspiration, peruse the views of successful bathrooms in the next two chapters. You'll see the latest in tubs and tiles, sinks and skylights, lighting and laminates. Soon you'll be on your way to creating the bathroom of your dreams.

A comfortable bedroom, a cheery two-sided fireplace, and a soothing whirlpool tub all team up in this spacious master suite. The bath continues around the corner. Elegant granite and cozy carpeting help tie areas together. Designer: Pulte Home Corporation.

7

TAKING STOCK

Before you jump into a bathroom shopping spree, take time to assess what you already have. A clear, accurate base map—such as the one shown below—is your best planning tool. It also helps you communicate both with design professionals and with showroom personnel.

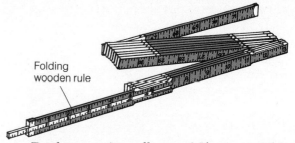

Folding wooden rule

Measure the space. To make your bathroom survey, you'll need either a folding wooden rule or a steel measuring tape. The folding rule (shown at right) is the pro's choice: it stays rigid when extended and is good for "inside" measurements.

First, sketch out your present layout (don't worry about scale), doodling in windows, doors, fixtures, and other features. Then measure each wall at counter height. Here's an example, using a hypothetical bathroom with the bathtub and door along one wall: beginning at one corner, measure the distance to the outer edge of the door, from there to the opposite edge of the door, from this edge to the bathtub, and across the bathtub to the corner. After you finish measuring one wall, total the figures; then take an overall measurement from corner to corner. The two figures should match. Measure the height of each wall in the same manner.

Do the opposite walls agree? If not, something's out of level or out of plumb; find out what it is. To check the room's corners, use a carpenter's square or employ the 3-4-5 method: measure 3 feet out from the corner in one direction, 4 feet in the other direction, and connect the points with a straightedge. If the distance is 5 feet, the corner is square.

Make a base map. Now draw your bathroom to scale on graph paper (most bathroom designers use ½-inch scale—1/24th actual size). An architect's scale is helpful but not really necessary. A T-square and triangle are all you need—plus some good drafting paper with ¼-inch squares.

The example shown below includes a centerline to the sink plumbing and electrical symbols—for outlets, switches, and fixtures. It's also helpful to note the direction of joists (see page 18), identify any bearing walls, and sketch in other features that might affect your remodeling plans.

A Sample Base Map

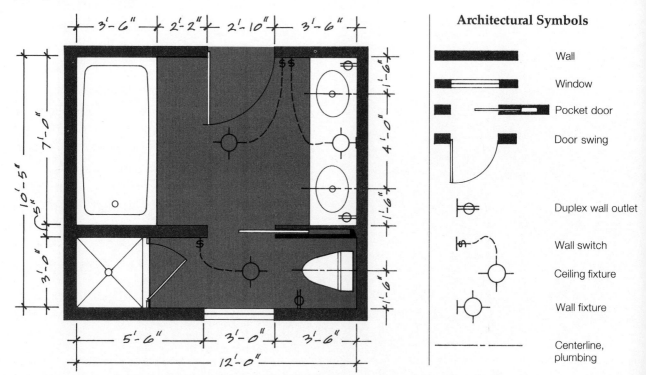

Architectural Symbols

Wall

Window

Pocket door

Door swing

Duplex wall outlet

Wall switch

Ceiling fixture

Wall fixture

Centerline, plumbing

A BATHROOM QUESTIONNAIRE

This questionnaire will help you to analyze present conditions in your bathroom as you begin to think about remodeling or adding another bath. When used with your base map, it also provides a good starting point for discussing your ideas with architects, designers, or bathroom showroom personnel. Note your answer to each question on a separate sheet of paper, adding any important preferences or dislikes that come to mind. Then gather your notes, any clippings you've collected, and a copy of your base map, and you're ready to begin.

1. What's your main reason for changing your bathroom?

2. How many people will be using the room? List adults, children, and their ages.

3. Are users left-handed? Right-handed? How tall is each one?

4. How many other bathrooms do you have?

5. What secondary activity areas would you like to include?
   ☐ Desk ☐ Garden ☐ Laundry facilities
   ☐ Exercise facilities ☐ Dressing or makeup area
   ☐ Sauna ☐ Spa

6. Are you planning any structural changes?
   ☐ Room addition to existing house ☐ Greenhouse window or sunroom ☐ Skylight ☐ Other

7. Is the bath located on the first or second floor? Is there a full basement, crawl space, or concrete slab beneath it? Is there a second floor, attic, or open ceiling above it?

8. If necessary, can present doors and windows be moved?

9. Do you want an open or vaulted ceiling?

10. What's the rating of your electrical service?

11. What type of heating system do you have? Does any ducting run through a bathroom wall?

12. Is the bath to be used by a physically challenged person? Is the individual confined to a wheelchair?

13. What is the style of your house's exterior?

14. What style (for example, high-tech, country contemporary, country French) would you like for your bathroom? Do you favor compartmentalized European layouts or a more open, informal look?

15. What color combinations do you like?

16. What cabinet material do you prefer: wood, laminate, or other? If wood, should it be painted or stained? Light or dark? If natural, do you want oak, maple, pine, cherry?

17. Storage requirements?
    ☐ Medicine cabinet ☐ Linen closet ☐ Drawers
    ☐ Cabinets ☐ Laundry hamper or chute
    ☐ Rollout baskets ☐ Open shelving ☐ Other

18. What countertop materials do you prefer?
    ☐ Laminate ☐ Ceramic tile ☐ Solid-surface
    ☐ Wood ☐ Stone ☐ Other. Do you want a backsplash of the same material?

19. List your present fixtures. What new fixtures are you planning? ☐ Bathtub ☐ Shower ☐ Tub/Shower combination ☐ Vanity ☐ Sink ☐ Toilet ☐ Bidet. What finish: white, pastel, full color?

20. Would you prefer natural or mechanical ventilation?

21. What flooring do you have? Do you need new flooring? ☐ Wood ☐ Vinyl ☐ Ceramic tile ☐ Stone ☐ Other

22. What are present wall and ceiling coverings? What wall treatments do you like? ☐ Paint ☐ Wallpaper ☐ Washable vinyl wallpaper ☐ Wood ☐ Faux finish ☐ Ceramic tile ☐ Other

23. Consider natural light sources: ☐ Skylight ☐ Window ☐ Clerestory

24. Artificial lighting desired: ☐ Incandescent ☐ Fluorescent ☐ Halogen ☐ 120-volt or low-voltage. What fixture types? ☐ Recessed downlights ☐ Track lights ☐ Wall-mounted fixtures ☐ Ceiling-mounted fixtures ☐ Indirect soffit lighting

25. What time framework do you have for completion?

26. What budget figure do you have in mind?

BASIC BATHROOM LAYOUTS

Now the fun begins: it's time to start planning your new bathroom. While brainstorming, it helps to have some basic layout schemes in mind. The floor plans shown below are both practical and efficient. Keep in mind that these layouts can be combined, adapted, and expanded to meet your needs. For additional ideas, see the floor plans in Chapter 2, "Case Studies."

Powder room. This two-fixture room, also known as a guest bath or half-bath, contains a toilet and a sink and perhaps some limited storage space. Fixtures can be placed side by side or on opposite walls, depending on the shape of the room. Very small sinks are available for extra-tight spaces.

Because the guest bath is used sporadically and for short intervals, it's a good place to enjoy more decorative but perhaps less durable finishes such as copper or upholstery. Since space may be tight, the door should swing open against a wall, clear of any fixtures. A pocket door may be the ideal situation.

Consideration should be given to privacy. Preferably, a guest bath should open off a hallway—not directly into a living, family, or dining room.

Family bath. The family bath usually contains three fixtures—a toilet, a sink, and a bathtub or shower or combination tub/shower. The fixture arrangement varies, depending on the size and shape of the room. Family baths often have cluster, or corridor, layouts; these should be at least 5 by 7 feet.

"Compartmentalizing" or separating fixture areas enables several family members to use the bathroom at the same time. A common arrangement is to isolate the toilet and shower from the sink and grooming area. This configuration can work well when adding a new bathroom isn't feasible.

The family bath is one of the most frequently used rooms in the house. Therefore, you'll want to choose durable, easy-to-clean fixtures and finishes.

Children's bath. Ideally, this bathroom is located next to the children's bedrooms so that each child has direct access.

Consider a single bath with two doors, or shared bathing and toilet facilities and an individual sink and dressing area for each child. When several children are sharing one bath, color coding of drawers, towel hooks, and other storage areas can help minimize territorial battles.

Sample Layouts

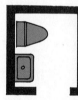

Powder room
4' by 4'-6"

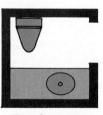

Powder room
5' by 5'

Powder room
3' by 6'

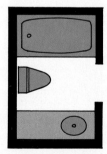

Family bath
5' by 7'

Family bath
7' by 11'

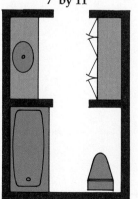

Family bath
8' by 12'

Back-to-back
5' by 7' each

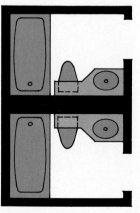

Children's baths require special attention to safety and maintenance. Single-control faucets will minimize the possibility of a hot-water burn; slip-resistant surfaces will minimize accidents. A timer on the light switch will keep your electrical bill down. Plastic-laminate counters and cabinets will prove durable and easiest to clean.

Master bath suite. The master bath has become more than just a place to grab a quick shower and run a comb through your hair. No longer merely a utilitarian space, today's master bath reflects the personality and interests of its owners. It includes dressing and grooming areas, toilet and bathing facilities, and other amenities. Fireplaces, whirlpool baths, oversize tubs, and bidets are often included in contemporary designs. Outside this bath is a natural place for a spa, sunbathing deck, or private garden.

Here are some "extras" you can plan into your master bath. Make sure that you provide adequate ventilation to prevent water damage (from splashes and condensation) to delicate objects and equipment.

■ *Exercise room.* Depending on space, you can set up everything from a space-efficient "ballet bar" to a fully-equipped in-house gym.

■ *Makeup center.* A well-lit area for makeup application and storage is an asset to almost any bath. The area could include an adjustable makeup mirror with magnification and its own light source (see page 92).

■ *Reading nook.* This might be the quietest refuge in the house. A cushioned bench with a good light source (maybe a skylight) is all you need for a few minutes of solitude. A small bookcase or magazine rack will be useful.

■ *Art gallery.* You can showcase works of art or build craft pieces, such as handmade tiles or a stained-glass window, right into the design.

■ *Greenhouse.* Because of the high moisture and humidity level, plants often thrive in a bathroom. It's an ideal place to bring a touch of nature into the house.

Barrier-free bath. If you are remodeling to accommodate a disabled or elderly person, be aware of this person's special needs. Minimum heights, clearances, and room dimensions may be required. For instance, to accommodate a wheelchair, the room must have specific clearances (see page 14). The door should swing out to allow easy movement in and out of the

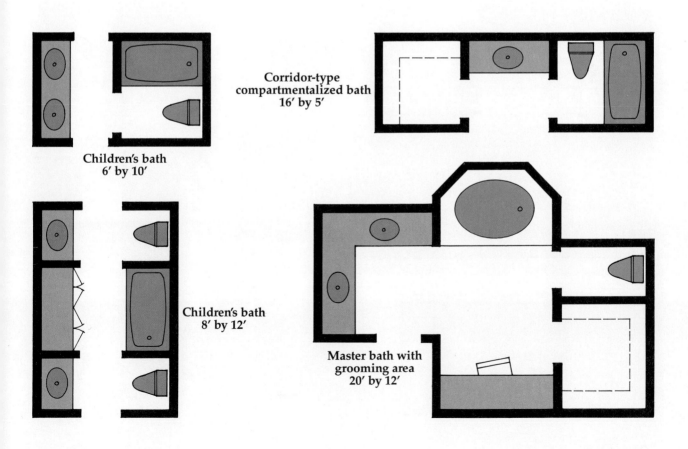

Children's bath
6' by 10'

Children's bath
8' by 12'

Corridor-type
compartmentalized bath
16' by 5'

Master bath with
grooming area
20' by 12'

Cabinet & Fixture Cutouts

To visualize possible layouts, first photocopy these scale outlines and cut them out. Move the cutouts around on a tracing of your floor plan (drawn to the same scale). Then draw the shapes onto the plan. It's easy to make your own cutouts for specialized fixtures and other features.

½ inch equals 1 foot

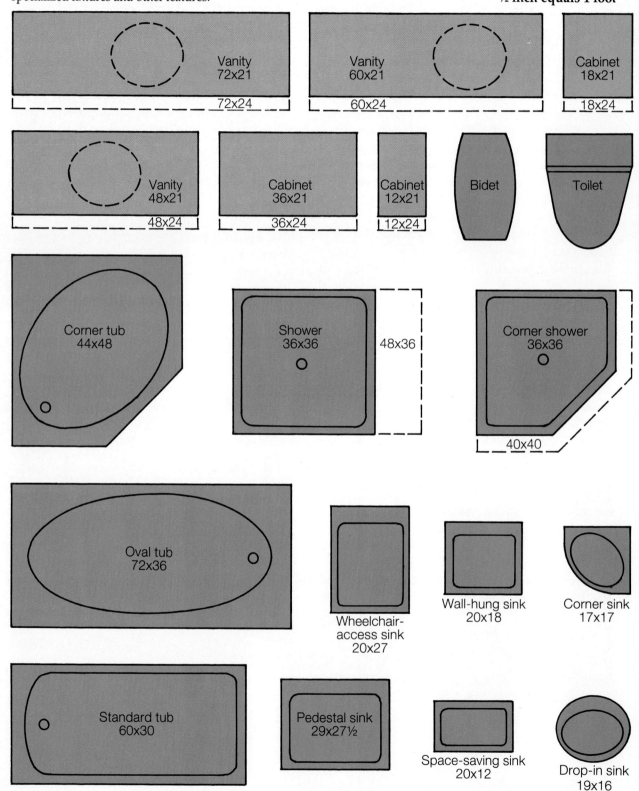

Vanity
72x21

72x24

Vanity
60x21

60x24

Cabinet
18x21

18x24

Vanity
48x21

48x24

Cabinet
36x21

36x24

Cabinet
12x21

12x24

Bidet

Toilet

Corner tub
44x48

Shower
36x36

48x36

Corner shower
36x36

40x40

Oval tub
72x36

Wheelchair-
access sink
20x27

Wall-hung sink
20x18

Corner sink
17x17

Standard tub
60x30

Pedestal sink
29x27½

Space-saving sink
20x12

Drop-in sink
19x16

room. The shower should be curbless so a wheelchair can roll in unobstructed. You may also want to install grab bars, use levers in place of door knobs, and choose fixtures and fittings specifically designed for the disabled.

ARRANGING FIXTURES

The more facts you have available, the easier it will be to work with your layouts. You'll keep costs down if you select a layout that uses the existing water supply, drain lines, and vent stack. If you're adding on to your house, try to locate the new bathroom near an existing bathroom or the kitchen. It's also more economical to arrange fixtures against one or two walls, eliminating the need for additional plumbing lines.

Generally, you can locate side-by-side fixtures closer together than fixtures positioned opposite each other. If a sink is opposite a bathtub or toilet, keep a minimum of 30 inches between them (see "Heights & Clearances" below).

To begin composing the layout, position the largest unit—the bathtub or shower—within the floor plan, allowing space for convenient access, for cleaning, and (if needed) for bathing a child.

Next, place the sink (or sinks). The most frequently used fixture in the bathroom, the sink should be out of the traffic pattern. Be sure to allow ample room in front for reaching below the sink; and give plenty of elbow room at the sides.

Locate the toilet (and bidet, if you have one) away from the door; often the toilet is placed beside the tub or shower. A toilet and bidet should be positioned next to each other. Don't forget about the swing-radius for windows and doors.

You'll probably experiment with several layouts before determining the best overall plan. Most likely, you'll have to make a compromise somewhere. If you identify your priorities clearly, it should be easy to choose the best solution.

HEIGHTS & CLEARANCES

There are standard minimum clearances in a well-planned bathroom. Community building codes specify minimum required clearances between, beside, and in front of bathroom fixtures to allow adequate room for use, cleaning, and repair. To help in your initial planning, check the minimum clearances shown at right.

Minimum Fixture Clearances

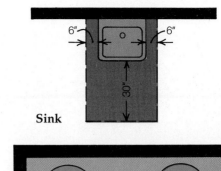

Sink

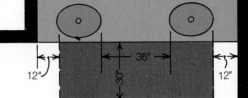

Double sink

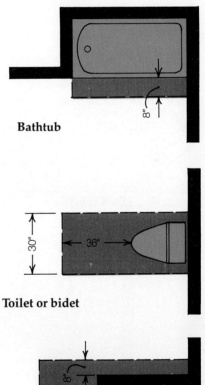

Bathtub

Toilet or bidet

Shower

Standard Heights

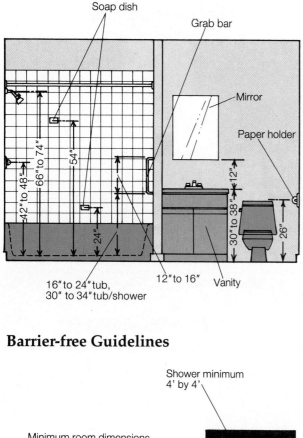

Soap dish

Grab bar

Mirror

Paper holder

42" to 48"

66" to 74"

54"

30" to 38"

12"

24"

26"

16" to 24" tub,
30" to 34" tub/shower

12" to 16"

Vanity

Barrier-free Guidelines

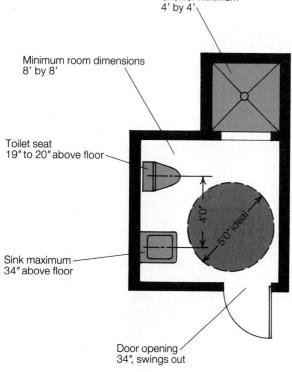

Shower minimum
4' by 4'

Minimum room dimensions
8' by 8'

Toilet seat
19" to 20" above floor

4'0"

5'0" ideal

Sink maximum
34" above floor

Door opening
34", swings out

Shown at top left are standard heights for cabinets, countertops, shower heads, and accessories. Recommended heights are steadily creeping higher, and you may wish to customize these to your own requirements.

Below left, we illustrate basic height and clearance guidelines for a barrier-free space.

A DESIGN CHECKLIST

Choosing appropriate fixtures, fittings, surfaces, lighting, and accessories is almost as important as determining a good layout. And don't forget storage space. Below, you'll find a quick checklist of bathroom components to consider. You'll find more information on each of these topics in Chapter 3, "A Shopper's Guide."

Fixture and fitting options. There's endless variety in bathroom fixtures and fittings. If possible, visit several showrooms to see the latest in tubs, showers, toilets, bidets, sinks, and faucets.

Surfaces. Floor, wall, and countertop surfaces should be durable as well as attractive. Wood, stone, tile, plastic laminate, solid-surface, glass, carpet, and resilient flooring are commonly used.

Saunas and steam showers. These luxurious features, once found mainly in gyms and health clubs, have recently entered the residential bathroom.

A sauna is a small wood-lined room (often sold prefabricated) that heats itself to around 200°F. Besides insulated walls, a solid-core door, and double-paned glass (if any), you'll also need an electric or gas sauna heater. Minimum size for a sauna is about 65 cubic feet per person.

New steam units are small enough to be housed in any number of handy locations—inside a storage cabinet, in an adjacent closet or alcove, or in a nearby crawl space. Besides the steam box, all you need is an airtight shower door, a comfortable bench, and effective ventilation.

Artificial light. Don't leave lighting as an afterthought; it should be part of the initial design. Today, there is a wide range of incandescent, fluorescent, and halogen light sources on the market, and a huge selection of fixtures to house them.

Natural light. Would your bathroom benefit by having additional natural light? You can achieve this by enlarging or adding a window or skylight. Windows on two adjacent walls provide more uniform lighting than a single source does.

Storage. While a powder room has minimal storage requirements, a family bath should include individual storage space for each family member, as well as places to keep cleaning supplies, paper products, soap, and incidentals. Vanities and other cabinets come with a variety of racks, shelves, pullouts, and lazy Susans, making limited storage space more efficient.

Today's bathrooms may also double as dressing and grooming areas as well; take time to consider these requirements. And how about a compact washer and dryer team, or a built-in ironing board?

Hardware and accessories. You'll be selecting door knobs, drawer pulls, towel bars, a toilet-paper holder, and other accessories. Though it may seem premature, you'll want to coordinate them with your fixtures, fittings, and surfaces to create an integrated overall look.

PLAYING IT SAFE

About 25 percent of all home accidents occur in the bathroom. You can reduce the risk of injury by precautionary planning.

For starters, be sure to select nonslip fixtures and surface materials. Anchor carpeting; choose rugs or bath mats with nonskid backing. Choose tempered glass, plastic, or other shatterproof materials for construction and accessories. Avoid mounting objects such as towel bars with sharp corners at eye level.

If children live in or visit your house, store medicines (and, when possible, household cleansers) in a cabinet with a safety latch or lock. Make sure that you can access the bathroom from the outside during an emergency.

Also be sure electrical receptacles are grounded and protected with GFCI circuit breakers. Outlets should be out of reach from the shower or bathtub. Keep portable heaters out of the bathroom. Install sufficient lighting, including a night light—especially if you have children.

Avoid scalding by lowering the setting on your water heater (see feature box at right), installing a temperature-limiting mixing valve, or a pressure-balanced valve to prevent sudden temperature drops.

Install L-shaped or horizontal grab bars, capable of supporting a person weighing 250 pounds, in tub and shower areas. Installation must be done properly—bracing between studs may be required. Plaster-mounted bars don't provide sufficient support.

WATER & ENERGY CONSERVATION

There are several simple conservation measures you can take in the bathroom. If you intend to replace fixtures and fittings, look at those specifically designed to save water and energy. Many manufacturers offer water-saving toilets, faucets, shower heads, and hand-held shower attachments at prices comparable to those of their conventional counterparts. Such fixtures and fittings can reduce both the amount of water used and the amount of energy needed to heat water for bathing.

Water-saving toilets use only about 3 gallons of water per flush, compared with 5 to 7 gallons used by conventional toilets. And now we have ultra-low-flush (ULF) models as well, which use only 1.6 gallons or less per flush. How much do ULFs really save over conventional toilets? Conservative estimates are 20 percent of total indoor water consumption for a family of four. Water-saving flushing devices can be installed on older toilets.

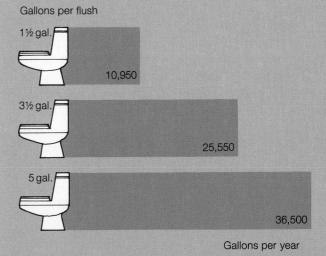

Gallons per flush

1½ gal. — 10,950

3½ gal. — 25,550

5 gal. — 36,500

Gallons per year

Some faucet and shower fittings include control devices that reduce flow while maintaining spray force. Others have aerators or fine mesh screens that break the water into droplets and disperse it over a wider area.

To save energy used for heating the bathroom and heating the water, make sure that the water heater, pipes, and walls are appropriately insulated. You can also save energy by reducing the water heater's temperature setting from the average 140°F to 110° or 120° (some dishwashers, though, require 160° water). If you're in the market for a new water heater, consider the energy-efficient models.

For more details on water- and energy-saving products, see Chapter 3, "A Shopper's Guide."

THE ELEMENTS OF DESIGN

Three visual keys to planning a balanced, pleasing bathroom design are line, shape, and scale. You'll need to think about each of these elements—as well as color, texture, and pattern—to achieve the overall look you want.

Line. Most bathrooms incorporate many different types of lines—vertical, horizontal, diagonal, curved, and angular. But often one predominates, and can characterize the design. Vertical lines give a sense of height; horizontals impart width; diagonals suggest movement; and curved and angular lines contribute a feeling of grace and dynamism.

Continuity of lines unifies a design. Try an elevation sketch of your proposed bathroom. How do the vertical lines created by the shower or tub unit, cabinets, vanity, windows, doors, and mirrors fit together? Does the horizontal line marking the top of the window match those created by the tops of the shower stall, door, and mirror?

Clearly, not everything can or should align, but the effect is far more pleasing if a number of elements do create a continuous line—particularly the highest features in the room.

Shape. Continuity and compatibility in shape also contribute to a unified design. Of course, you needn't repeat the same shape throughout the room—carried too far, that becomes a monotonous proposition.

Study the shapes created by doorways, windows, countertops, fixtures, and other elements. Look at patterns in your flooring, wall covering, shower curtain, and towels. Are they different or similar? If similar, are they boringly repetitive? Consider ways to complement existing shapes or add compatible new ones; for example, you might echo an arch over a recessed bathtub in the shape of a doorway, or in shelf trim.

Scale. When the scale of bathroom elements is in proportion to the overall size of the room, the design feels harmonious. A small bath seems even smaller if equipped with large fixtures and a large vanity. But the same bath can look larger or at least in scale if fitted with space-saving fixtures, a petite vanity, and open shelves.

Consider the proportions of adjacent features as well. When wall cabinets or linen shelves extend to the ceiling, they often make a room seem top-heavy—and therefore smaller. To counteract this look without losing storage space, place cabinet doors or shelves closer together at the top. Let your floor plan and elevation drawings suggest other ways you can modify the scale of different elements to improve your design.

Color. The size and orientation of your bathroom, your personal preferences, and the mood you want to create all affect color selection. Light colors reflect light, making walls recede; thus, a small bath treated with light colors appears more spacious. Dark colors

A Sample Elevation

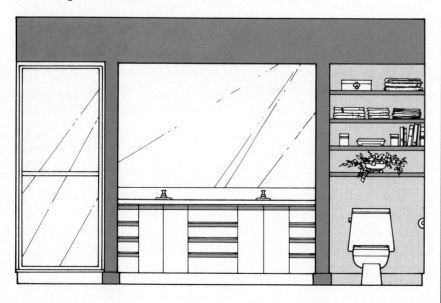

Alignment of horizontal planes shows how line creates a harmonious design. Notice the relationships among lines along the wall and within each compartment. For example, the toilet tank top and vanity door tops are at the same height; and the first shelf is aligned with the towel bar on the shower.

absorb light and can visually lower a ceiling or shorten a narrow room.

When considering colors for a small bathroom, remember that too much contrast has the same effect as dark color: it reduces the sense of spaciousness. Contrasting colors work well for adding accents or drawing attention to interesting structural elements. But if you need to conceal a problem feature, it's best to use one color throughout the area.

Depending on the orientation of your bathroom, you may want to use warm or cool colors to balance the quality of the light. While oranges, yellows, and colors with a red tone impart a feeling of warmth, they also contract space. Blues, greens, and colors with a blue tone make an area seem cooler—and larger.

A light, monochromatic color scheme (using different shades of one color) is restful and serene. Contrasting colors add vibrancy and excitement to a design. But a color scheme with contrasting colors can be overpowering unless the tones of the colors are varied.

After you narrow down your selections, make a sample board to see how your choices work together. Color charts for various fixtures are readily available, as are paint chips, fabric swatches, and wallpaper and flooring samples.

Remember that the color temperature and intensity will also be affected by the placement of light fixtures. (For details, see pages 89–91.)

Texture and pattern. Textures and patterns work like color in defining a room's style and sense of space. The bathroom's surface materials may include many different textures—from a glossy countertop to wood cabinets to a quarry-tile floor.

Rough textures absorb light, make colors look duller, and lend a feeling of informality. Smooth textures reflect light and tend to suggest elegance or modernity. Using similar textures helps unify a design and create a mood.

Pattern choices must harmonize with the predominant style of the room. Although we usually associate pattern with wall coverings or a cabinet finish, even natural substances such as wood, brick, and stone create patterns.

While variety in texture and pattern adds interest, too much variety can be overstimulating. It's best to let a strong feature or dominant pattern be the focus of your design and choose other surfaces to complement rather than compete with it.

Designing with Color

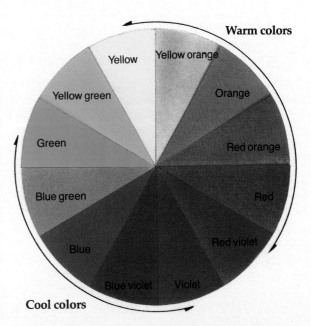

As a rule, work with colors that are adjacent on the color wheel; save complementary colors—those opposite one another—for accents.

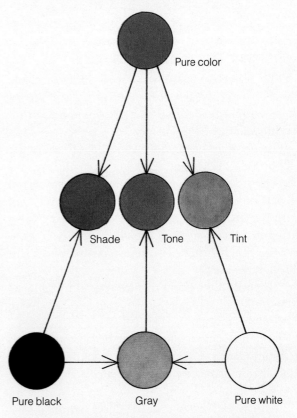

This pyramid shows how hues are created. Shades are made by adding black to pure color, tones by adding gray, and tints by adding white. Gray is a mixture of pure black and pure white.

Structural Framing

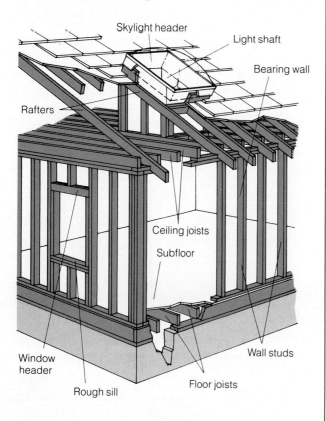

Skylight header
Light shaft
Bearing wall
Rafters
Ceiling joists
Subfloor
Window header
Rough sill
Floor joists
Wall studs

Plumbing

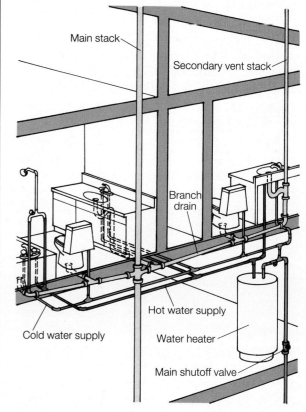

Main stack
Secondary vent stack
Branch drain
Hot water supply
Cold water supply
Water heater
Main shutoff valve

STRUCTURAL CHANGES

If you're planning to open up a space, add a skylight, or recess a tub or shower into the floor, your remodel may require some structural modifications.

As shown above, walls may be either *bearing* (supporting the weight of ceiling joists and/or second-story walls) or *nonbearing*. If you're removing all or part of a bearing wall, you must bridge the spot with a sturdy beam and posts. Nonbearing (also called *partition*) walls can usually be removed without too much trouble—unless pipes or wires run through the area.

Doors and windows require special framing, as shown. Skylights require similar cuts through ceiling joists and/or rafters.

A standard doorway may not be large enough to accommodate a new tub or whirlpool. If you're remodeling, make sure you can get such a large fixture into the room.

Hardwood, ceramic, or tile floors require a very stiff underlayment. You may need to beef up the floor joists and/or add additional plywood or particleboard subflooring on top.

PLUMBING RESTRICTIONS

Your plumbing system is composed of two parts: a water-supply system, which brings water to the house and distributes it, and a drain-waste-ventilation (DWV) system, which removes water and waste.

Every house has a main soil stack. Below the level of the fixtures, it's the primary drainpipe. At its upper end, which protrudes through the roof, the stack becomes a vent. To minimize costs and keep the work simple, arrange a fixture or group of fixtures so they are as close to the present pipes as possible.

A proposed fixture located within a few feet of the main stack usually can be vented directly by the stack. Sometimes a fixture located far from the main stack will require its own branch drain and a secondary vent stack (a big job). Be sure to check your local plumbing codes for exact requirements.

Generally, it's an easy job—at least conceptually—to extend existing hot- and cold-water supply pipes to a new sink or fixture. But if you're working on a concrete slab foundation, you'll need to drill through the slab or bring the pipes through the wall from another point above floor level.

Electrical Wiring

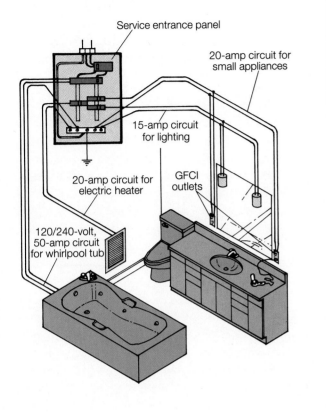

Service entrance panel

20-amp circuit for small appliances

15-amp circuit for lighting

20-amp circuit for electric heater

GFCI outlets

120/240-volt, 50-amp circuit for whirlpool tub

Mechanical Systems

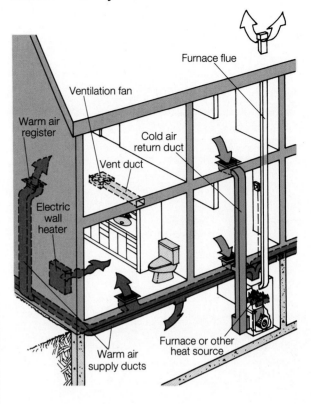

Furnace flue

Ventilation fan

Warm air register

Cold air return duct

Vent duct

Electric wall heater

Furnace or other heat source

Warm air supply ducts

ELECTRICAL REQUIREMENTS

When planning your new bathroom, take a good look at the existing electrical system. Most houses today have both 120-volt and 240-volt capabilities. But older homes with two-wire (120 volts only) service of less than 100 amps probably can't supply the electricity needed to operate a new whirlpool tub, sauna, steam generator, or electric heater. You may need to upgrade your electrical system.

The National Electrical Code (NEC) requires that all bathroom outlets must be protected by ground fault circuit interrupters (GFCI) that cut off power immediately if the current begins leaking anywhere along the circuit. If you're adding a new wall, you may be required by code to add an outlet every 12 feet or one per wall. In addition, codes may strictly dictate the placement of outlets, appliance switches, and even light fixtures in wet areas.

While it's possible to locate electrical wiring inside conduit that is surface-mounted, it is preferable to enclose all wires within the walls. But before finalizing your plan, determine what plumbing pipes, heating ducts, and other electrical wires are already concealed there.

HEATING & VENTILATION

Unless the bath contains a heating duct and register, you'll need to determine how to extend the supply and return air ducts (a major undertaking) to connect with the rest of your central system. Since you'll be using the bathroom only intermittently, you may wish to provide an auxiliary heat source rather than depend on your central system. A small wall- or ceiling-mounted heater can provide all the warmth you need.

All gas heaters require a gas supply line and must be vented to the outside, so you'll probably want to locate a gas heater on an exterior wall. Otherwise, you'll have to run the vent through the attic or crawl space and the roof. (For options and details on heaters, see pages 80–81.)

Ventilation is critical. Even if you have natural ventilation, you may want to consider adding forced ventilation. In a windowless bathroom, a fan is required by code. It's important that your exhaust fan have adequate capacity, rated in cubic feet per minute (CFM). The fan should be capable of exchanging the air at least eight times per hour. (For more information, see page 81.)

DOLLARS & CENTS

How much will your new bathroom cost? According to the National Kitchen & Bath Association, the average figure is $9,087. This is, of course, only the sketchiest of estimates. You may simply need to replace a countertop, add recessed downlights, or exchange a worn-out bathtub to achieve a satisfying change. On the other hand, the sky is the limit: extensive structural changes coupled with ultra-high-end materials and fixtures can easily add up to $40,000 or more.

As shown below, labor typically eats up 29 percent of the pie; cabinets come in at around 24 percent; and, on the average, fixtures and fittings add another 18 percent. Structural, plumbing, and electrical changes all affect the bottom line significantly.

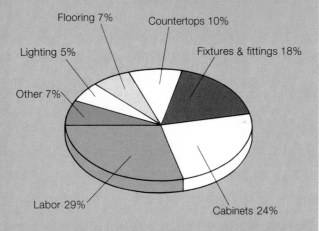

Flooring 7% · Countertops 10% · Lighting 5% · Fixtures & fittings 18% · Other 7% · Labor 29% · Cabinets 24%

How do you keep the budget under control? For starters, know if you're looking at a simple face-lift, a more extensive replacement, or a major structural remodel. Fixture, fitting, and materials prices vary greatly. Shop for ballpark figures in different categories, mull them over, then present your architect or designer with a range of options and a bottom line with which you can be comfortable.

What about the fees of design professionals? Expect to be charged either a flat fee or a percentage of the total cost of goods purchased (usually 8 to 10 percent). General contractors will include their fee in a final bid.

Don't make price your only criterion for selection, however. Quality of work, reliability, rapport, and on-time performance are also important. Ask professionals for the names and phone numbers of recent clients. Call several and ask them how happy they were with the process and the results. Some might allow you to come and take a look at the finished work.

WORKING WITH PROFESSIONALS

The listing below covers professionals in bathroom design and construction and delineates some of the distinctions (although there's overlap) between architects, designers, contractors, and other professionals.

Architects. Architects are state-licensed professionals with degrees in architecture. They're trained to create designs that are structurally sound, functional, and aesthetically pleasing. They also know construction materials, can negotiate bids from contractors, and can supervise the actual work. Many architects are members of the American Institute of Architects (AIA). If structural calculations must be made, architects can make them; other professionals need state-licensed engineers to design structures and sign working drawings.

So is an architect the number one choice for designing your bathroom? Maybe yes, maybe no. If your new remodel involves structural changes, an architect should be consulted. But some architects may not be as familiar with the latest in bathroom design and materials as other specialists.

Bathroom designers. A bathroom designer is a specialist in bathrooms. They know the latest trends in fixtures and furnishings, but may lack the structural knowledge of the architect and the aesthetic skill of a good interior designer (see facing page).

If you decide to work with a bathroom designer, look for a member of the National Kitchen & Bath Association (NKBA) or a Certified Bathroom Designer (CBD). Both associations have codes and sponsor continuing programs to inform members about the latest building materials and techniques.

Retail specialists. This category includes showroom personnel, building-center staff, and other retailers. Some are quite qualified and genuinely helpful. But others may be motivated simply to sell you more goods. If your bathroom requires only a minor face-lift, this kind of help may be all you need. If you're tackling a larger job, check the specialist's qualifications carefully.

Typically, you provide a rough floor plan and fill out a questionnaire; the retailer provides a finished plan and/or materials list—*if* you buy fixtures or other goods. Some firms do the work by computer simulation, others the traditional way.

Interior designers. Even if you're working with an architect or bathroom designer, you may wish to call on the services of an interior designer for finishing touches. These experts specialize in the decorating and furnishing of rooms and can offer fresh, innovative ideas and advice. And through their contacts, a homeowner has access to materials and products not available at the retail level. Many designers belong to the American Society of Interior Designers (ASID), a professional organization.

As bathroom design becomes more sophisticated, professionals become more specialized. A prime example is the lighting design field, which has come into its own in recent years. A lighting designer specifies fixtures and placement of the lighting for your new bathroom and works with the contractor or an installer to make the new lighting scheme a reality.

General contractors. Contractors specialize in construction, although some have design skills and experience as well. General contractors may do all the work themselves, or they may assume responsibility for hiring qualified subcontractors, ordering construction materials, and seeing that the job is completed according to contract. Contractors can also secure building permits and arrange for inspections as work progresses.

When choosing a contractor, ask architects, designers, and friends for recommendations. To compare bids, contact at least three state-licensed contractors. Give each one either an exact description and your own sketches of the proposed bathroom or plans and specifications prepared by an architect or designer. Be precise about who will be responsible for what work.

Subcontractors. If you act as your own contractor, you will have to hire and supervise subcontractors for specialized jobs such as wiring, plumbing, and tiling. You'll be responsible for permits, insurance, and payroll taxes, as well as direct supervision of all the aspects of construction. Do you have the time or the knowledge required for the job? Be sure to assess your energy level realistically.

Warm and woody, or classic white: the choice is yours. At top right, 1 by 6 clear redwood paneling is accented by glass block and stainless steel vanity top. Below, clean white columns and connecting arch frame a classic marble-trimmed tub surround.

ARCHITECT: KURT B. ANDERSON/ANDARCH ASSOCIATES

CASE STUDIES

There's nothing like a picture book when you're shopping for inspiration. In this light, we present the following gallery of bathroom designs.

These 18 studies present as broad a range of styles as possible. You'll find small baths, larger ones, and luxurious master suites. Some homeowners wrestled with an existing architectural footprint; others looked up and out; a few borrowed space from an unused adjacent room. All sought to make the space as pleasingly useful as possible. As one master-suite owner commented, "All we need now is a hot plate."

One of these solutions may seem just right for your situation. Or, you may simply wish to incorporate one or more of the design elements or fixtures you see here; in this case, check "A Shopper's Guide" (beginning on page 61) for details.

New and old combine to bring the best of both worlds to this bath. A modern whirlpool tub meets turn-of-the-century wood wainscoting and marble; chrome accessories glow with soft filtered light from etched windows and mirrors. Interior designer: Paul Vincent Wiseman.

TRADING PLACES

The remodeling agenda for this space called for flip-flopping the existing bathroom and dressing room. Besides efficiency and convenience, the homeowners wanted elegance, a rich sense of color, and a touch of drama—all without the room being too dark.

Custom tiles set the tone; forest green is accented by a band of carnelian chevrons. Sand is embedded in the floor tiles for slip-proof footing. Walls are sponged and streaked with paint. A new ceiling soffit, lit by decorative strip lights, gives the room a lifted look. Custom wall sconces and low-voltage tub downlights round out the lighting scheme.

From the shower, it's just a few steps to the oversize dressing room, abundantly fitted with cedar-lined racks, drawers, and cubbyholes.

Designer: Osburn Design.

The main view (above) shows flush-mounted "one-and-a-half-person" whirlpool tub below window to private garden; tub spout, faucet handles, and hand shower are all housed on the deck. Nearby are his-and-her sinks and vanities, plus a two-person walk-in shower (upper left). Bird's-eye maple cabinets have angled drawers (facing page) and appliance garages (left).

STEPS & SQUARES

This second-story master bath continues *step* and *square* motifs found throughout a house that uses classic materials with contemporary sophistication. Blue granite squares cover floor and shower. Walls are sponged and ragged in white, gray, blue, and lavender paint, their texture and coloring a softer echo of the granite. Square windows with etched square insets allow owners to see out, but protect privacy. The built-in wall unit—stepped, of course—provides generous storage as well as display space.

Two dressing rooms open off the entrance passage. A separate toilet compartment has a sandblasted window of its own. Downlights and skylights yield balanced light throughout; custom wall sconces repeat the step-and-square pattern once more.

Architect: House + House of San Francisco.

The granite-lined step-down bath/shower makes use of "found space" from a lowered portico downstairs. A bench below the spout creates a waterfall effect as tub is filled.

Squares abound in the sink area (facing page), viewed here from the adjacent master bedroom. Square-etched square windows, square skylights, granite squares, and wall sconces all contribute; and mirrored surfaces multiply the effect. Stepped storage units (above) connect sink area and shower; niches provide room for art and collectibles.

NIGHT & DAY

More and more homeowners are opting for multiroom bath layouts, incorporating such amenities as dressing areas, makeup centers, and separate "wet" areas. This bathroom, part of a complete basement-level suite, is really two distinct rooms: one a bright, light-catching vanity area, the other a quieter, more introverted bathing space.

The main vanity room includes double sinks, a lowered makeup counter, mirrors aplenty, and cozy white wool carpeting. The bath area has a whirlpool tub, walk-in shower, toilet, and pedestal sink in an arched recess. Sealed marble flooring is lifted to wainscot level; the upper walls and ceiling have faux marble painting. The rosy band of light is from neon concealed by a soffit.

Architect: Remick Associates.

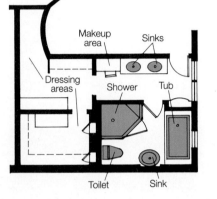

Bright outer room, with columns of lights like rising bubbles, has twin sinks, makeup area, lots of mirrors. Cabinets feature custom-crafted fluting, shaped from 1⅝-inch poplar; they support Spanish marble countertops. At back is entrance to his-and-her dressing areas.

Dramatic lighting (above) accents inner bath. Low-voltage halogen downlights are controlled by pinhole apertures; indirect neon accent light glows behind ceiling soffit. All light fixtures are dimmer-controlled, allowing many options. Bath layout (left) includes walk-in shower, toilet alcove, and pedestal sink, plus spacious whirlpool tub.

ANTIQUES & ORCHIDS

This several-room remodel not only makes ample space for soaking and dressing, but showcases the owners' antiques collection as well. The elegant whirlpool bath forms a hub; a limestone-lined shower and separate toilet compartment are nearby. His-and-her grooming areas, with separate sinks and dressing rooms, radiate out in both directions.

Time-honored elements in the basic design scheme consist of antique furniture pieces, pewter accessories, French flooring pavers with limestone accents, and limestone tub trim and countertops. Curved soffits with built-in downlights are a contemporary contribution. Graceful orchids, placed here and there throughout the suite, add a finishing touch.

Interior designer: Ruth Soforenko Associates. Building designer: Joseph Bellomo.

Separate areas radiate from a central hub containing shower and whirlpool tub. His sink (left), behind small sitting area, includes modern frameless cabinets and a dressing room (visible in vanity mirror). Her makeup center (above), adjacent to shower, gains a personal look from collection of antique linens and dressing table accessories.

Large whirlpool tub (above) is central focus of two bath wings. Built-in neck roll allows relaxed soaking; blinds provide privacy; wall sconces add drama at night. Flooring detail (left) shows used French pavers with smaller limestone accents. The rustic tiles include many casual irregularities—even chickens' footprints in one unit.

This bath gains style from easy-to-clean marble squares on the floor and walls (above). (To handle their weight, floor joists needed reinforcing.) European pedestal sinks and wraparound storage unit look trim, save space. An adjacent storage and laundry room (right) takes pressure off the small bath.

REGARDING THE BASIC SQUARE

How can you update a nondescript 7½- by 8-foot bathroom? And one that's a "walkthrough," or major traffic corridor, as well? In this case, out went the clunky old tub and shower; in came hard-working, compact fixtures and a wraparound sink-and-storage unit. Fixtures were placed to maximize space while keeping the traffic pattern clear. An adjacent room works to stretch the bath space, housing large floor-to-ceiling storage cabinets plus a compact European washer and dryer.

How to let more light in? The designer added a large splayed skylight, painted it terra cotta for a dash of color, and placed low-voltage strip lights in the soffits for a nighttime accent. Both color and light bring out a subtle warmth in the sand-toned sealed marble tiles.

Designer: Ellen Alvarez/Design Cabinet Showrooms.

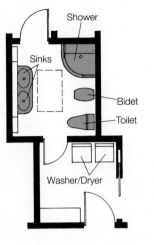

Sleek European shower unit (below) has adjustable shower head and massage unit, plus fold-down seat; its curved sliding doors can be removed for cleaning. View past the shower toward laundry (below left) shows space-saving but stylish bidet and toilet.

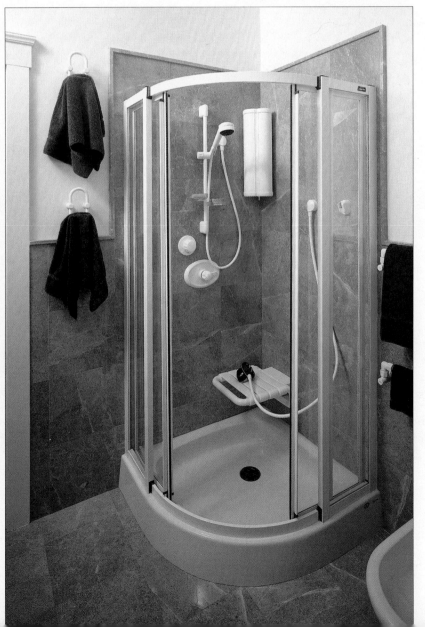

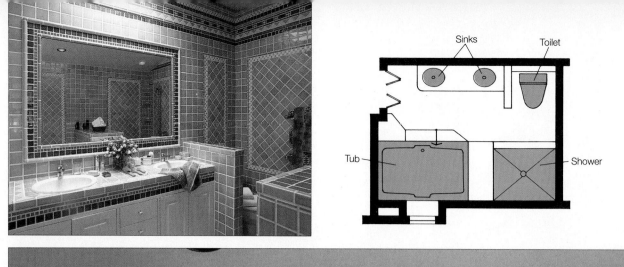

Sinks Toilet

Tub Shower

M ILES OF TILES

It's the tilework that's the showstopper, but the rest of this master bath-room works hard, too. The owners found enough room for a whirlpool tub, double shower, matching sinks, and some built-in storage. Knee walls separate fixtures, yet maintain a sense of openness in the other-wise small space.

Tiles are a festival of color, but artfully laid out: elements include 1- to 6-inch squares and triangular border pieces. A skylight brings in some sunlight, and a recessed window niche frames a vase full of flow-ers. The original ceiling was raised to slope upward from the tub area to the vanity.

Designers: Marc Rebarchik and Brett Heller.

The view toward the master bedroom (left) features whirlpool tub, built-in laundry and linen cabinets, and plenty of colorful tile details. View from door (above) shows twin sinks, toilet partition, and heated towel rack. A white vanity cabinet (facing page, top) forms a clean counterpoint to tile details; the walk-in shower is visible in the mirror.

ON THE ROCKS

The owners had enjoyed using the outdoor shower at an isolated cabin and wanted to bring that experience back home. When their children moved out, they opted to stay put—and build a fantasy-fulfilling master bath in the space where a bedroom and small bath had been.

Boulders went in first. Then the bathroom was literally built around them. The two-sided fireplace took the place of one house wall, so a structural beam was added to support the roof. A new arched skylight brings in plenty of daylight; spotlights come into play at night. Past the sliding glass doors, it's only a few steps to the hot tub. And outdoors, more boulders, pine trees, and a carpet of aromatic pine needles continue to evoke the alpine spirit.

Architect: Obie Bowman.

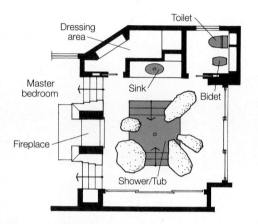

Dressing area

Toilet

Master bedroom

Sink

Bidet

Fireplace

Shower/Tub

The new master bath lies just beyond a bedroom sitting area with a two-sided fireplace (below); fire's light flickers in both spaces.

Giant granite boulders (facing page) surround the shower area, focal point of this outdoorsy master suite. Twin heads (above) provide plenty of shower power; the recess may be spout-filled for a more leisurely soak. For further comfort, bathroom slab has radiant heating below.

A FAR EASTERN JOURNEY

Part of an overall oriental house design, this master bathroom suite includes an efficient dressing room, vanity and makeup alcove, toilet compartment, and a raised bath area complete with a deep Japanese-style soaking tub.

Shoji panels and wood accents are of beautiful vertical-grain fir; the panels fit right over original aluminum windows. Wall coverings employ three paper patterns, plus a separate border; off-white ceilings and gray-white wool carpeting form a clean, uncluttered background. When the bathroom is not in use, additional shoji panels close it off from the adjacent bedroom.

Interior designer: Lequita Vance-Watkins/adVance Design of Carmel.

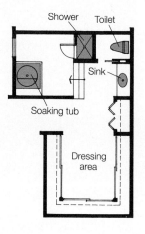

Dressing area (below) is lined with storage spaces, some faced with mirrors. Replacing closet louvers, shoji paper maintains Japanese flavor while allowing air circulation. Acrylic-lined panels conceal the warm-fluorescent ceiling fixtures.

Sink and makeup area (above) features black lacquer cabinets, enameled sink, and bulb-framed mirror. Clerestory windows bring in natural light. The toilet compartment is nearby. Up two steps are the Japanese-style soaking tub (facing page) and a conventional shower stall.

Sinks

Shower

Dressing area

Toilet

A TOUCH OF GLASS

Precautions about glass houses don't necessarily apply to bath-rooms—at least not to beautifully translucent walls like these. Eight-inch glass blocks form a stepped partition that secludes a comfortable walk-in shower. Glass blocks also admit light through the end wall and into an adjacent toilet alcove.

The layout is basically L-shaped, but nothing's simply square: the main bath area tapers and curves at the same time; the dressing area, which links bath to bedroom, shoots off at a sharp angle. Triangular glass pendants and diagonally set floor tiles introduce interesting angles to the main bath.

Architect: Laurence Allen.

Stepped glass-block partition (left) defines large walk-in shower; glass blocks in exterior walls let in softly diffused light. Twin sinks are set off by green marble countertop and backsplash; they sit atop trim gray European-style cabinets. Enameled fixed head and massage unit (facing page, top left) provide shower spray; controls (facing page, top right) are mounted to glass at shower entrance. Dressing area (above) has built-in dressers, marble counters, warm wool carpeting. More glass blocks screen the toilet alcove.

LOOKING UP FOR LIGHT

As shown in this marble-tiled space, *small* and *comfortable* are not mutually exclusive terms. There's a lot of careful organization at work in this compact corridor layout: the built-in whirlpool tub and steam shower fit along one wall; the toilet and a vanity with double sinks line the opposite wall.

The architect looked up for light and interest, creating an "escape route" for the eye in this otherwise landlocked room. Large mirrors behind the vanity reflect the skylight as well as the pale marble, enhancing the feeling of space.

Although the area is small, it makes room for such amenities as a built-in TV, telephone, heated towel bar, and heat lamp.

Architect: Ted T. Tanaka.

Toilet

Sinks

Steam shower

Tub

Compact whirlpool tub and steam shower (facing page) occupy one side of marble-lined bath. Sculptural light well attracts eye upward. Vanity area (right) includes two sinks and built-in TV; mirrors help stretch sense of light and space. Heated towel bar (above) is one of many finishing touches.

GABLE-END GLAMOUR

The slopes of a second-story dormer presented obvious remodeling challenges. But instead of fighting the angles, the architect chose to highlight them: note the ceiling planes, the angular shower alcove, and the step motif on the tub partitions. Adjacent crawl spaces became opportunities for cleverly designed storage and dressing areas.

The owners wanted to maintain the traditional feel of their older home. The cabinetry and tub wainscoting respect this requirement, as do the chrome hardware and the pendant light fixture. Shuttered windows admit light but allow privacy, as do the glass-block partitions. Indirect uplighting, built into the partitions, creates a soft wash of light at night.

Architect: Remick Associates.

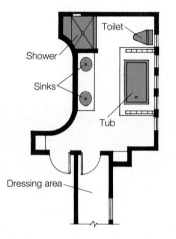

A whirlpool tub (facing page) is the centerpiece of this bath: its marble deck, raised-panel wainscoting, and glass-block partitions establish a reposed, traditional style. The tub's styling repeats in the storage-generous vanity (right). A built-in shower (above) fits under the steeply pitched roof of the dormer.

ETCHINGS & ANGLES

When the kids moved away, an upstairs bedroom and tiny bath made way for this calm, uncrowded bathroom. A large octagonal skylight is its centerpiece; the lines of shower, storage alcove, toilet compartment, and vanity all play off that.

The basic space is L-shaped, with entry through the vanity area. There's a step up to the main bath and a step down at the shower (which looks flush, but actually drops off several inches to corral water).

Quiet, closely coordinated colors and textures establish a background of repose. Custom etching on the walk-in shower provides an elegant but undistracting accent. A floor-to-ceiling mirror stretches space visually and reflects shower details. Pinpoint lighting throughout the tub and shower area comes from low-voltage MR-16 downlights with slot apertures.

Designers: Rick Sambol/Kitchen Consultants and Lynne Shilling.

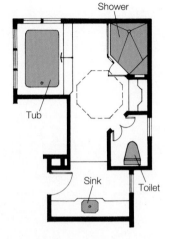

Stylish European storage unit (below), toilet compartment (behind doors), and twin sinks embellish this bath. Gray-white wall fabric leads into carpeted vanity area, which features mirror-mounted wall sconces, stylish sink, limestone countertop, and more angled cabinets.

The octagonal central skylight (facing page) is the form around which this bathroom is disposed; its screened top opens for bug-free ventilation. A seamless-looking etched glass shower (above) continues the play of angles. Gray limestone squares decorate both floor and walls.

Exercise room

Tub

Steam shower

Toilet

Dressing area

Makeup area

Sinks

Dressing area

Toilet

Alternating patterns of lighter and darker marble give visual interest to the main bath area (below), which contains both a whirlpool tub and a walk-in steam shower. Glass blocks provide wavery light and color, but maintain privacy. A mirrored exercise room (left), complete with TV/video alcove, is just a few steps away.

A FITNESS CENTER FOR TWO

In this master suite, owners can take a turn on the exercise machines, cool down on an adjacent deck, then soothe sore muscles in the steam shower or whirlpool tub. The T-shaped space features "his-and-her everything": matching sinks, separate dressing rooms, a two-person tub, two shower heads (one lower than the other), and two toilet compartments. Space for this exercise and bathing center was borrowed from an unused bedroom.

A vanity corridor with generous mirror and counter space (plus a separate makeup alcove opposite the sinks) links the inner bath with the bedroom. Dressing rooms branch off this central area.

Designer: Rick Sambol/Kitchen Consultants.

Bright, light-colored vanity area (above) links inner bath with bedroom. Existing ceiling was raised and skylight and plant niche were added. White wool carpeting is cozy on chilly mornings.

BACK TO BACK

Compress a family of four (including two teenagers) into a narrow Victorian row house with one small, quirky bathroom, and you're asking for trouble. Solution? The designers carved two hard-working baths, each with a distinct personality, out of a none-too-generous existing space.

The new adult bath, which stole a little room from the adjacent bedroom, revolves around stylish but space-saving vanity areas. Behind the shower, glass blocks receive daylight from an existing light shaft (painted white to boost reflectivity). Behind the tub, etched glass windows provide more light.

The teenagers' bath is even smaller. Here, a space-saving storage unit occupies the wall above the sink and toilet; an open shower design and an etched glass window maximize the sense of space and light.

Designer: Osburn Design.

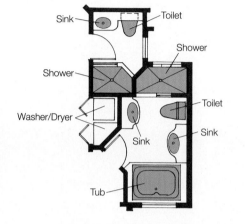

Colorful tile enlivens teenagers' bath (at left). Custom vanity surrounds sink and toilet, incorporating mirrors and wall sconces. Cabinets are whitewashed birch with textured rubber door panels; countertop and backsplash are solid-surface material in a gray stone pattern. Shower (above, reflected in mirror) has tiled knee-wall base for panel of clear glass.

Adult bath layout (above) makes use of every inch. Sink alcoves with 12-inch-deep storage cabinets and cantilevered German sinks fit between built-in shower enclosure and compact whirlpool tub (shown at left). Like the window glass, the bathroom door is also frosted—so light can flow unimpeded from one space to another.

A SPLIT-LEVEL SUITE

This bathroom comes in two installments: the molded whirlpool tub is at master-bedroom level; nearby, down a set of stylish stairs, is the bathroom proper.

The tub sits atop its own oak pedestal, offering a leisurely soak within easy range of the bed. Nearby windows give bathers an ocean view. A skylight well, interior wall openings, and track lighting contribute architectural punch.

The downstairs vanity area features vertical-grain fir cabinets, a laminate countertop, recessed sinks, and a trim fluorescent bar fixture. There's lots of built-in storage, plus a separate shower, in the right-angle wing beyond the vanity.

Architect: Obie Bowman.

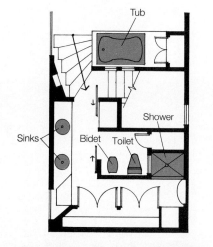

Molded whirlpool tub (facing page) and TV monitor built into part-wall above it are focal points of high-ceilinged master bedroom. Laundry chute is incorporated into tub's oak deck. Offset steps and rail (above) wind down a level to vanity (left) and toilet compartment. The massive wooden doors to these areas slide on galvanized barn hardware.

View from the shower bench (right) takes in whirlpool tub, wall-mounted tub fittings, vanity area, and, beyond bathroom door, a wet bar area with sink, microwave oven, and under-counter refrigerator.

Shower
Dressing area
Makeup area
Bidet
Tub
Toilet
Sinks
Wet bar

M

ARBLE REFLECTIONS

The owners wanted lots of marble, so their architect gave them walls, floor, and countertop of bluish green stone, set off by black fixtures, cabinets, and accessories. A long strip skylight lets in filtered daylight, providing soft modeling to otherwise shiny, dark surfaces. Uninterrupted stretches of mirror amplify the play of colors, light, and angles almost endlessly.

The vanity holds twin sinks and a built-in makeup niche. There's ample storage below the countertop, and mirrors conceal shelved cabinets recessed in the wall. A private toilet compartment has a bidet nearby. Three steps down is the dramatic shower, complete with built-in benches. Four watertight light fixtures, tucked into the skylight, add a soft glow at night.

Architect: Daniel H. Levin. Design: Harry H. Kahn.

Vanity and tub areas (left) show off 12-inch marble tiles, given additional drama by black cabinets, fixtures, and accessories. Large mirrors reflect steep angles, skylight, frosted bulbs; makeup alcove mirrors conceal storage area (the mirrored fronts open with touch latches). The room steps down to a large shower (above) with marble bleacher-bench.

PRETTY IN PINK

Clean white woodwork, hand-painted tile, and subtle pink wallpaper distinguish this fastidiously detailed bath. The walk-in shower rises through the room's center: white columns, wainscoting, crown moldings, and the peaked ceiling all give it visual importance.

Matching grooming areas occupy opposite walls. Each includes a tile countertop and ceramic sink, a raised-panel vanity cabinet, an oval mirror, and candelabra wall sconces. The window-wrapped tub, nestled into a frame-and-panel pedestal, commands a cheery garden view. Double doors on the fourth wall lead to a spacious dressing room.

Architect: Remick Associates.

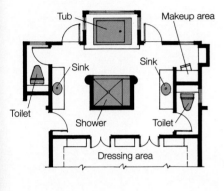

A freestanding walk-in shower (above) is the centerpiece of this four-sided bath layout. Looking past one grooming area (facing page), you see the wooden tub pedestal and a garden view. Route between tub and shower (upper left) leads to dressing table (lower left) with lowered countertop, three-sided mirror, and supplementary lighting.

WOOD CURVES

It's not hard to see that these homeowners love both wood and curves. In their private bath-retreat, straight lines were avoided, whenever possible, in favor of rounded corners and curved soffits and ceilings. To keep the design as clean as possible, built-in drawers and compartments were set flush, and nearly invisible: all pulls, hinges, and electrical outlets and switches are concealed. Even vent fans are housed behind routed slots in the upper wall paneling.

A cedar-lined sauna, double steam shower, built-in TV, and adjacent outdoor hot tub make this retreat very comfortable. A long stretch of built-in closets helps make it efficient, too.

Architect: Raymond L. Lloyd. Design: Michael Assum/Mark Twisselman.

Steam shower

Sauna

Sinks

Toilet

Closets

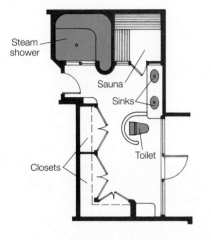

This master bath (facing page) showcases beautiful woods and fine craftsmanship. Tamboured wall slats and larger crosspieces are mahogany; curved pieces were steamed for 24 hours, then bent to shape. The countertop (above) was fashioned from a massive walnut slab; faucets have digital temperature controls. Compact cedar-lined sauna (upper left) houses several benches, plus electric sauna heater. Uplights accent area above zebrawood-and-koa closets (lower left).

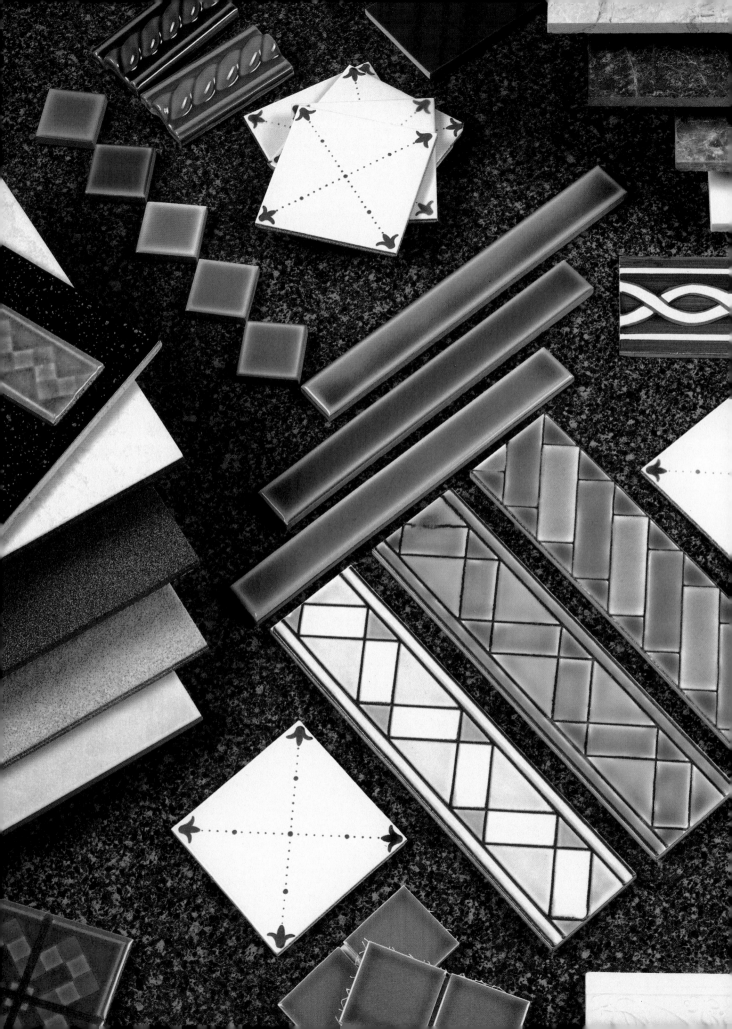

A SHOPPER'S GUIDE

Once upon a time, you simply purchased a white pedestal sink, a 30- by 60-inch tub, a toilet, and a mirrored medicine cabinet and called it a bathroom. But all that has changed: today, there are integral solid-surface sinks; freeform acrylic whirlpool tubs; one-piece, ultra-low-flush toilets. And that's just the beginning. How can the inexperienced bathroom shopper cope?

That's where this chapter can help. Color photographs show the latest in styles. And text and comparison charts give you the working knowledge to brave the showrooms, to communicate with an architect or designer, or simply to replace that dingy, old-fashioned wall tile.

For names and addresses of manufacturers of many of the products we show, see the listings on pages 94–95.

Here's a small sampling of new tile choices; they're set against a background of granite-like laminate. We show mostly accent pieces, including 1-inch-square inlays, hand-painted trim strips, mosaics, and rope borders. Twelve-inch tiles at far left are ceramic "stone"; large units at upper right are real marble.

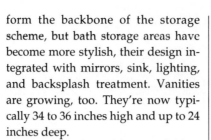ABINETS

It wasn't so long ago that "bathroom storage" meant a clunky medicine cabinet above the pedestal or wall-hung lavatory sink. Then along came boxy vanities, and the bathroom acquired a bank of drawers to one side of the plumbing compartment.

Today, as changing life-styles find new expression and bathrooms become grooming centers, exercise gyms, and spas, storage needs and configurations are also changing. One or more base vanities may still form the backbone of the storage scheme, but bath storage areas have become more stylish, their design integrated with mirrors, sink, lighting, and backsplash treatment. Vanities are growing, too. They're now typically 34 to 36 inches high and up to 24 inches deep.

Like kitchens, bathroom cabinet layouts are now more sophisticated. Perhaps you'll wish to curve a custom unit around a corner, let built-ins form knee walls between use areas, or plan a floor-to-ceiling storage column.

On the following pages, we describe the two ways all cabinets are constructed and the three ways you can purchase cabinets. We also show a variety of cabinet styles and storage options.

Cabinet Close-ups

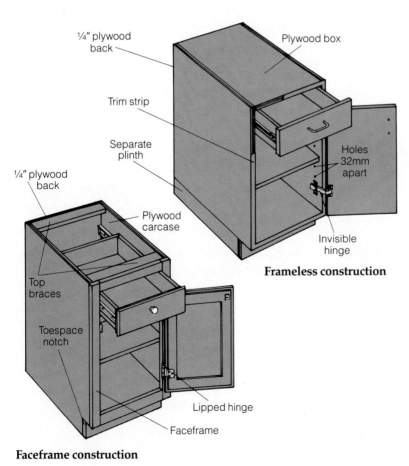

¼" plywood back

Trim strip

Separate plinth

¼" plywood back

Plywood box

Holes 32mm apart

Invisible hinge

Frameless construction

Plywood carcase

Top braces

Toespace notch

Lipped hinge

Faceframe

Faceframe construction

Traditional or European-style?

Traditional American cabinets mask the raw front edges of each box with a 1-by-2 "faceframe." Doors and drawers then fit in one of three ways: flush; partially offset, with a notch; or completely overlaying the frame. The outer edges of the faceframe can be planed and shaped (called "scribing") to conform to individual requirements. But the frame takes up space; it reduces the size of the door opening, so drawers or slide-out accessories must be significantly smaller than the width of the cabinet.

Europeans, whose homes are often so small that every inch of space counts, came up with "frameless" cabinets. A simple trim strip covers raw edges, which butt directly against one another. Doors and drawers usually fit to within ¼ inch of each other, revealing a thin sliver of the trim. Interior components—such as drawers—can be sized larger, practically to the full dimension of the box.

Another big difference: frameless cabinets typically have a separate toespace pedestal, or plinth. This allows you to set counter heights specifically to your liking, stack base units, or make use of space at floor level.

Stock, custom, or custom modular?

Cabinets are manufactured and sold in three different ways. The type you choose will affect the cost, overall appearance, and workability of your bathroom.

Stock cabinets. Buy your bathroom "off the shelf" and you'll save—if you're careful. Mass-produced, standard-size cabinets are the least expensive option, and they can be an excellent choice if you clearly understand the cabinetry you need. You

Vanity cabinets are still the hub of many bath designs, but styles and layouts are becoming more varied all the time. Custom modular unit (above, left) sports the "unfitted" look of fine furniture. Freestanding oak vanity (above, right) features diagonal mirror dividing twin sink areas. At right, shallow built-ins with tambour-faced sliding doors help stretch space in a tiny bath.

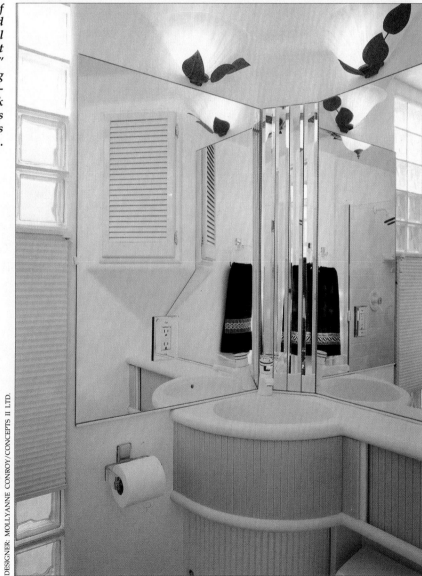

may find stock lines heavily discounted at some home centers.

As the name implies, the range of stock sizes is limited. Even so, you can always specify door styles, which direction doors swing, and whether side panels are finished. And you can sometimes get options and add-ons such as pullouts or laundry bins.

As today's bath serves more grooming functions, it may incorporate traditional closet and bureau units. The dressing room below links master bedroom with bath proper, features maple built-ins with lots of nooks and crannies.

Custom cabinets. Many people still have a cabinetmaker come to their house and measure, then return to the cabinet shop and build custom frame carcases, drawers, and doors.

Custom shops can match old cabinets, size oddball configurations, and accommodate complexities that can't be handled with stock or modular cabinets. Such work generally costs considerably more than medium-line stock or modular cabinets.

Custom modular cabinets. Between stock and custom cabinetry are "custom modular cabinets" or "custom systems," which can offer the best of both worlds. They are

manufactured, but they are of a higher grade and offer more design flexibility than stock cabinets. Not surprisingly, they cost more, too.

You can change virtually everything on these basic modules: add sliding shelves; replace doors with drawers; add wire bins, hampers, and pullouts. If necessary, heights, widths, and depths can be modified to fit almost any design.

Judging quality

To determine the quality of a cabinet, look closely at the drawers. They take more of a beating than any other part of your cabinets.

DESIGNER: FONTENOT DESIGNS

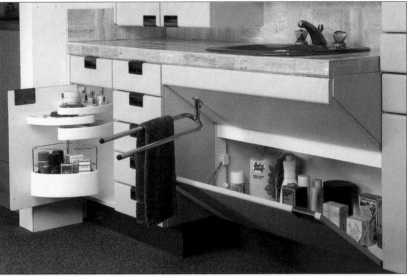

Mirrored cabinet above is a sleek update of standard medicine cabinet, with built-in incandescent strip lights and interior amenities. Euro-style unit (above, right) demonstrates the range of storage accessories available with some cabinet lines. Floor-to-ceiling column (right) can hold a lot—even a swiveling TV.

Drawer guides and cabinet hinges are critical hardware elements. Check for adjustability; they should be able to be reset and fine-tuned with the cabinets in place. And make sure laminate and edge banding are thick enough so they won't peel at the corners or edges.

Shopping around

If you've done some homework, you can get a quote for cabinets relatively easily. But options alter price dramatically—so the same basic cabinet can end up costing a range of prices.

When you buy cabinets, part of what you're paying for is planning help. Some retailers and designers will give you a questionnaire (much like the one on page 9) to assess your needs. Your current base map (see page 8) is the best aid you can offer a designer. In some showrooms, computer renderings help customers visualize the finished bathroom—in which case, prices for different cabinets are just a keystroke away.

ARCHITECT: REMICK ASSOCIATES

COUNTERTOPS

After being steamed and splashed, good countertop materials still come up shining because they're moisture resistant (or better yet, waterproof). The best materials are less likely to scratch or chip.

What are your choices?

Plastic laminate, ceramic tile, solid-surface acrylics, and stone are the four major countertop materials in current use. Synthetic marble, popular in past years, is losing ground to solid-surface materials. Wood is sometimes used for countertops, too; but to prevent water damage, the surface of wood countertops should be finished with a sealant.

When shopping, you probably won't be able to compare all the materials in one place. Some dealers

---

COMPARING COUNTERTOPS

Plastic laminate

Advantages. You can choose from a wide range of colors, textures, and patterns. Laminate is durable, easy to clean, water resistant, and relatively inexpensive. With the right tools, you can install it yourself.

Disadvantages. It can scratch, chip, and stain, and it's hard to repair. Conventional laminate has a dark backing that shows at its seams; new solid-color laminates, designed to avoid this, are somewhat brittle and more expensive.

Cost. Standard brands cost $1 to $3.50 a square foot; premolded, particleboard-backed tops in limited colors are $5 to $10 per running foot. Installed, a custom countertop with 2-inch lip and low backsplash costs from $40 to $90 per running foot (more for solid-color materials).

Ceramic tile

Advantages. It's good-looking; comes in many colors, textures, and patterns; and is heatproof, scratch resistant, and water resistant if installed correctly. Grout is also available in numerous colors. Patient do-it-yourselfers are likely to have good results.

Disadvantages. Many people find it hard to keep grout satisfactorily clean. Some designers recommend using less grout space (1/32 inch versus the typical 1/4 inch), though the thinner joint is definitely weaker. You can also buy grout sealers, but their effectiveness is disputed. A hard, irregular surface can chip glassware. High-gloss tiles show every smudge.

Cost. Prices range from 50 cents to $50 per square foot. Choose nonporous glazed tiles, which won't soak up spills and stains. Installation costs vary, depending on tile type and size of job (generally, the smaller the countertop, the higher the per-foot price).

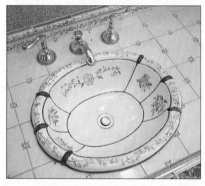

ARCHITECT: REMICK ASSOCIATES

Solid-surface

Advantages. Durable, water resistant, heat resistant, nonporous, and easy to clean, this marble-like material can be shaped and installed with woodworking tools (but do it very carefully, or cracks can occur, particularly around cutouts). It allows for a variety of sink installations, including integral units like the one shown on page 69. Blemishes and scratches can be sanded out.

Disadvantages. It's expensive, and requires very firm support below. Until recently, color selection was limited to white, beige, and almond; now imitation stone and pastels are also available.

Cost. For a 24-inch-deep counter with a 2-inch front lip and 4-inch backsplash, figure $100 to $150 per running foot, installed. Uninstalled, it's about half that. Costs go up for wood inlays and other fancy edge details.

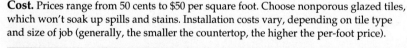

with showrooms are listed in the yellow pages under Countertops or Kitchen Cabinets & Equipment; they'll probably have tile, plastic laminate, solid-surface products, and—maybe—wood. Large building supply centers carry plastic laminate, synthetic marble, and wood. For other dealers or fabricators, check listings in the categories Marble—Natural; Plastics; and Tile. Designers and architects can also supply samples of materials.

Backsplash fever

These days, bathroom designers are also using the backsplash—the wall surface surrounding the countertop proper—to make an aesthetic statement. A good backsplash also has practical advantages: if properly installed, it seals this vulnerable area from moisture, and it makes the wall a lot easier to keep clean.

Just a few years ago, the average countertop, usually laminate, included a 4-inch lip on the back. Today's backsplashes are higher and often feature materials found there alone. Geometric or hand-painted accent tiles are popular choices. Stone tiles make an economical alternative to solid granite or marble. Solid-surface materials are a natural here, too. Glass block and mirrors are other options.

Need more inspiration? The photographs in "Case Studies" (beginning on page 23) present a wide variety of treatments to consider.

COMPARING COUNTERTOPS

DESIGNER: DESIGN TIMES TWO

Synthetic marble

Advantages. This group of man-made products, collectively known as "cast polymers," includes cultured marble, cultured onyx, and cultured granite. All three are relatively inexpensive and easy to clean. Many colors are available. Cultured onyx is more translucent than cultured marble. These products are often sold with an integral sink. You can color-coordinate a synthetic marble top with tub, shower, and wall panels.

Disadvantages. Synthetic marble is not very durable, and scratches and dings are hard to mend (the surface finish is usually only a thin veneer). Backings are typically porous. Quality varies widely; look for Cultured Marble Institute or IAPMO certification.

Cost. A cultured marble top with 4-inch backsplash averages about $25 to $30 per running foot. Figure $35 per foot for onyx, and add another 25 percent for cultured granite. Sometimes an integral sink is included in the price; sometimes it's extra.

Wood

Advantages. Wood is handsome, natural, easily installed, and easy on grooming accessories and glassware.

Disadvantages. Untreated, wood will discolor, warp, stain, and decay if exposed to water. If you use wood, thoroughly protect it on all sides with a good sealer such as polyurethane. Pay particular attention when sealing the joints so moisture won't cause hidden damage underneath the wood.

Cost. Maple butcher block, the most popular ready-made top, costs about $12 to $16 per square foot for 1½- to 1¾-inch thickness. Installed cost is $50 and up per running foot, including miters and cutouts. It's sold in 24-, 30-, and 36-inch widths. Edge-joined oak, redwood, sugar pine, and teak are also used for counters.

DESIGNER: RON HELMS

DESIGNER: CHARLOTTE BOYLE INTERIORS
ARCHITECT: J. ALLEN SAYLES

Stone

Advantages. Granite and marble, both used for countertops, are beautiful natural materials. In most areas, you'll find a great selection of colors and figures. Stone is water resistant, heatproof, easy to clean, and very durable.

Disadvantages. Oil, alcohol, and any acid (even chemicals in some water supplies) can stain marble or damage its high-gloss finish; granite can stand up to all of these. Solid slabs are very expensive. Some homeowners and designers use stone tiles— including slate and limestone—as less expensive alternatives.

Cost. A custom-cut marble slab costs $40 to $70 per square foot (with granite about $60 and up)—polished and finished with a square or slightly beveled edge. Decorative details add more. Installation costs about $75 an hour.

SINKS & FAUCETS

No longer just a basin and a mirror, the sink area has become a carefully orchestrated environment for grooming and personal care. Layouts with two sinks—housed in one continuous vanity, in side-by-side alcoves, or in matching configurations on opposite walls—are a common sight. Some bathrooms also include a separate, smaller wash basin in the toilet compartment or makeup area.

Sinks and faucets have become design accents in their own right—a comparatively low-commitment way to add a bit of dash to an otherwise restrained design scheme. (If you later decide you don't like the boldness, it's a lot simpler to change a faucet than shower or tub surround.)

Sink options, new & old

Sinks are available in a huge array of styles, shapes, materials, and finishes. You can make the sink stand out—or blend its look with that of a period-

DESIGNER: RUTH SOFORENKO ASSOCIATES

DESIGNER: SHELLEY MASTERS

style tub, shower, or toilet fixture. Whether for an antique or ultramodern design, some sink manufacturers can provide custom colors on special orders.

Deck-mounted sinks. The vanity-bound fixture is still the most practical arrangement. You'll find a wide selection of materials in deck-mounts: vitreous china, fiberglass-reinforced plastic, enameled cast iron, and enameled steel are most common. Fiberglass is lightweight and moderately priced, but tends to scratch and dull. Vitreous china

DESIGNER: PATRICK SHERIDAN

DESIGNER: SHELLEY MASTERS

The sink area—with vanity, countertop, backsplash, mirror, and light fixtures—offers a major decorating opportunity, and deck-mounted sinks are the choice in most design schemes. Wood sink and countertop (top left) were laminated from clear redwood, then carefully sealed. Steel sinks (top right) star in bold contemporary bath. Black china basin (right) sets off fire-red tiles. Integral solid-surface sink (far right) offers easy maintenance. Pewter-look model (facing page) blends with antique accents.

(made with clay that's poured into molds, fired in a kiln, and glazed) is heavy, comes in many colors, and is easy to clean; it also resists scratches, chips, and stains. Enameled cast iron is more expensive and durable than vitreous china or enameled steel, but is very heavy. An enameled steel surface is easy to clean and lighter and less expensive than vitreous china or enameled cast iron—but also much less durable.

Brass and copper sinks are strikingly elegant as accents. But they require zealous maintenance, so you may want to reserve them for powder rooms, guest baths, or other low-use areas.

You also have a choice of mounting methods with various deck-mounted models. *Self-rimming* sinks with molded overlaps are supported by the edge of the countertop cutout; *flush* deck-mounted sinks have surrounding metal strips to hold the basin to the countertop; *unrimmed* sinks are recessed under the countertop and held in place by metal clips.

Integral-bowl sinks. A solid-surface countertop (see page 66) can be coupled with a molded, integral sink for a sleek, sculpted look. Sink color can either match the countertop or complement it; for example, you might choose a cream-colored sink below a granite-patterned counter. Edge-banding and other border options abound. Other integral sinks come in synthetic marble, vitreous china, and fiberglass.

A countertop with integral bowl has no joints, so installation and cleaning are easy. The one-piece molded unit sits on top of a vanity or cabinet; predrilled holes are part of the package.

Pedestal sinks. Pedestal sinks are making a big comeback, in a wide range of traditional and modern designs. Typically of vitreous china,

these elegant towers are easy to install and clean around; the pedestal usually hides the plumbing. Some models have old-style vanity legs.

Pedestal sinks are typically among the highest-priced basins. Another disadvantage: there's no storage space under the basin.

Wall-hung sinks. Like pedestals, wall-hung sinks are enjoying a con-

ARCHITECT: KURT B. ANDERSON/ANDARCH ASSOCIATES

Pedestal and wall-hung sinks are newly popular. Matching marble pedestal sinks (top) are set off by arches, columns; popular white Eurostyle model (far right) has brash red accents; more traditional pedestal (right) utilizes awkward corner area. Compact wall-hung sink (middle) has space-saving side-mount faucet.

temporary revival. Materials and styling are along the same lines; in fact, some designs are available in either version.

Wall-hung sinks come with hangers or angle brackets for support. Generally speaking, they are the least expensive and most compact sink options, and relatively easy to install. If you're putting in a wall-hung model for the first time, plan to tear out part of the wall to add a support ledger.

Faucets

The world of sink faucets is constantly changing, presenting new colors, shapes, styles, and accessories. Finishes include bold enamel, traditional brass, shiny chrome, soft pewter, and elegant gold.

You can choose a showstopper in boldest modern or most quaintly antique styling; coordinate with tub and shower fittings; or pick the same handles for all fixtures in the room. You can buy faucets with digital temperature readouts, scaldproof models, and spouts that stop the flow when your hand is removed. How about a swiveling European faucet with an adjustable spray and a gum-massage attachment?

Sink faucets are available with single, center-set, or spread-fit controls. A single-control fitting has a combined faucet and lever or knob controlling water flow and temperature. A center-set control has separate hot and cold water controls and a faucet, all mounted on a base. A spread-fit control has separate hot and cold water controls and a faucet, independently mounted. Pop-up or plug stoppers are sold separately or with the faucet and water controls.

Two questions to ask when evaluating clever, streamlined designs: How well could you work the controls with soaped-up hands and sleep-bleared eyes? And how easy would it be to clean or maintain the installation?

Whatever style you choose, most bathroom professionals agree that solid-brass construction is the best way to go. Ceramic- or nylon-disk designs are generally easier to maintain than older washer schemes.

When you select your sink, be sure the holes in it will accommodate the type of faucet you plan to buy, as well as any additional accessories.

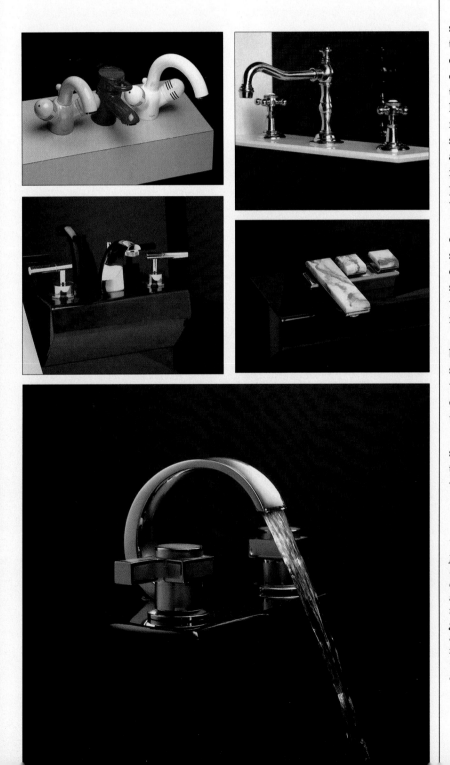

There's a faucet for every taste— from brightly colored enamels (top left) with adjustable sprays and accessories to elegant antique brass styles (top right). Twin-lever chrome model (middle left) meets barrier-free guidelines; marble-trimmed "side-saddle" design (middle right) offers new twist. Twin-handle gold faucet (bottom) exemplifies graceful new curved designs.

TUBS & FITTINGS

In many bathrooms, the tub is the focus of the room, a gratifying symbol of luxury and relaxation. In new installations, whirlpool tubs—now available in more traditional tub styles and sizes—are in high demand. Put a whirlpool on a platform; wrap windows around it (if privacy is a concern, see page 88); let a skylight beam down some sunshine or starlight; mount built-in speakers for soft background music: the tub becomes a destination in its own right. But for on-the-go workday bathing, a separate shower, unless space prohibits, is a nearly universal request.

Tub choices

The market overflows with bathtub styles. The 30- by 60-inch tub, which often controlled the dimensions of the 5- by 7-foot bathroom, no longer rules the buyer. Tubs come in new and more comfortable shapes and sizes and are available in a wide range of colors.

The basic bathtub. The boxy, familiar tub is enameled steel, relatively inexpensive, and lightweight—but noisy, cold, and prone to chipping. Built-to-last enameled cast-iron tubs are more durable and warmer to

Here are traditional tub styles that withstand the test of time. Stout freestanding old-timer with reconditioned chrome spout and handles (right) highlights brand-new bathroom. Japanese soaking tub (above) is focal point of a cedar-lined open bath.

Oval-shaped pedestal tub (above) is trimmed with solid-surface deck and redwood skirting; it's nestled into corner of garden bath. Want more traditional styling? Recessed tub alcove (right) blends Victorian wainscoting, wallpaper, marble, and tub fittings with up-to-the-minute whirlpool tub.

the touch, but very heavy (they may require structural reinforcement). They're manufactured in many colors.

Rectangular tubs come in two styles: recessed and corner. Recessed tubs fit between two side walls and against a back wall; they have one finished side. Corner models have one finished side and end and may be right- or left-handed. A 72-inch-long model is better than the standard 60 inches, if space allows; a depth of 16 inches or more is more comfortable than the standard 14.

Square tubs are commonly 4 by 3½ or 4 feet; often they include an integral seating ledge. Square tubs are manufactured for both recessed and corner installation.

The age of plastics. The most innovative tubs these days are usually plastic—either vacuum-formed acrylic or injection-molded thermoplastics like ABS. These lightweight shells are easy to transport and retain heat well.

But best of all is their range of contours and sizes. Plastic tubs are available in neutrals and in the latest colors—from soft pastels to glossy black. The one drawback: those shiny, elegant-looking surfaces tend to scratch or dull easily.

These tubs are usually designed for platform or sunken installation. Built-in features vary.

Freestanding tubs. An old-fashioned freestanding tub, such as the enduring clawfoot model, makes a nice focal point for a traditional or country design. You can buy new reproductions or a reconditioned original. Such tubs can double as showers with the addition of Victorian-inspired shower-head/diverter/curtain rod hardware.

Looking for traditional fixtures and fittings? Recently, many new sources for renovators' supplies have sprung up: check specialty shops and antique plumbing catalogs.

Whirlpool tubs. Think of these hydromassage units simply as bathtubs with air jets. Unlike an outdoor spa, the whirlpool uses a standard hot-water connection; once your soak is over, the water is drained.

A motor, pump, and jets are what make the whirlpool go. Jet designs vary: generally, you can opt for high volume and low pressure (a few strong jets) or low pressure and high volume (lots of softer jets). Typically, the more jets, the easier it is to pinpoint an aching body part—though some users find these setups less comfortable. The best whirlpools are adjustable—for water volume, air-water mixture, and direction.

Looking for extras? Consider adding digital temperature controls, timers, built-in fill spouts, or cushy neck rolls for comfort.

Because of their extra weight, whirlpool tubs may need special floor framing. They may also require an extra-capacity main water heater or separate in-line heater.

Soaking tubs. Soaking tubs, like Japanese *furos* (made of wood), have deep interiors. Ideal for small spaces, they come in recessed, platform, and corner models, with rectangular or round interiors of fiberglass or acrylic.

Hot tubs, which use a wooden barrel-design and continuous water supply, can present moisture problems in all but the best-ventilated spaces. They are probably best confined to a deck or private garden.

Tub fittings

For tubs and tub/showers, you can use either single or separate controls. Tubs require a spout and drain. Tub/showers need a spout, shower head (see page 77), diverter valve, and drain. These may be deck- or wall-mounted, or a combination. The best fittings are made of brass and come in several finishes, including chrome, pewter, gold, and enamel. You'll also find color-coordinated pop-up drains and overflow plates.

Ever had a tub spout poke you while you were trying to relax? Mount it along the back wall or deck. Position handles where you can get to them easily, such as at the front and slightly to one side. Roman or waterfall spouts are striking-looking and fill tubs much faster than standard fittings.

Unfortunately, tubs, especially whirlpools, aren't great for really getting *clean*. For that, add a separate hand shower controlled by a nearby diverter valve.

Fill 'er up! Waterfall spouts handle oversize tubs in a hurry. The one at top is flanked by diverter and hand shower. Wall-mounted spout (middle left) adds a touch of brass. Modular fixture handles (middle right) can complement a sculptural tub spout (bottom right). A hand shower (bottom left) brings flexibility—and a cleansing spray—to your tub environment.

ARCHITECT: REMICK ASSOCIATES

SHOWERS & FITTINGS

DESIGNER: DEBRA GUTIERREZ

Choose a shower with a zoomy, free-standing European surround or a custom built-in with decorative glass doors—or, if there's space, one with no doors at all. We've seen showers recessed into a wall, tucked under a steep roof, or nestled into an out-of-the-way corner. We've also seen showers that serve as an architectural centerpiece around which an entire bath revolves.

Most people prefer an open, light shower environment. Seamless glass doors and surrounds are popular. Glass block can let in soft light while maintaining privacy. And how

Seamless-look walk-in shower (below) blends right into an upstairs loft. The shower at far right is both beautiful and barrier-free—incorporating an adjustable hand-held shower head, vertical grab bar, and comfortable bench into a stylish marble design.

ARCHITECT: LYNDON/BUCHANAN ASSOCIATES; DESIGN: DIANE MCKENZIE/JOHN HALLEY

about a skylight above, with decorative accent lighting taking over at night?

Your basic choices

You can select a prefabricated shower stall, match separate manufactured components, or build completely from scratch. Think about amenities you might enjoy: a comfortable bench or fold-down seat; adjustable or hand-held shower heads; room for appliances and shaving equipment; sturdy grab bars.

Prefabricated shower stalls. If you have oversize doors in your house, you may be able to use a one-piece molded shower or tub/shower surround in a remodel. However, these units are designed for new houses or additions. Popular units are available in fiberglass-reinforced plastic, acrylic, plastic laminate, and synthetic marble. Some have ceilings. For comfort, choose a shower that's at least 3 feet square.

The term "shower stall" needn't mean something boxy and boring—or even economical. The high-end Eurostyle units are doing away with all that. Circular, corner, and angular

wraparounds are available with enough spray heads and accessories to please the most demanding shower connoisseur. Circular showers often have clear or tinted acrylic doors that double as walls.

Build your own. You can also mix and match surround, base, and doors to create the shower of your choice.

Custom shower surrounds require solid framing for support. You can add prefabricated wall panels or use a custom wall treatment such as ceramic tiles, natural or synthetic marble, or a solid-surface material. Molded fiberglass wall panels may include molded soap dishes, ledges, grab bars, and other accessories.

A shower base can be purchased separately or in a kit that includes the shower surround. Most bases are made of fiberglass, acrylic, or terrazzo and come in standard sizes in rectangular, square, or corner configurations with a predrilled hole for the drain. It's easy to find a base that matches a tub or other fixtures, as many manufacturers make both—in many colors. Of course, you can also have a professional float a custom mortar base and line it with tile.

Doors for showers come in a variety of styles: swinging, sliding, folding, and pivoting. For tub/showers, choose sliding or folding doors. Doors and enclosures are commonly made of tempered safety glass with aluminum frames. These frames come in many finishes; you can select one to match your fittings. The glazing can be clear, hammered, pebbled, tinted, or striped. The seamless look is popular, though expensive. Glass designs require more maintenance; some homeowners keep a squeegee nearby for daily cleaning.

ARCHITECT: HOUSE + HOUSE OF SAN FRANCISCO

This total shower environment revolves around a high-power dome head; a column-mounted hand shower helps with washing duties. Neon in the ceiling soffit matches pale lavender in wall plaster. Weep holes, windows, and an overhead vent fan keeps things aired out.

Swinging, folding, or pivoting doors can be installed with right or left openings. Folding doors are constructed of rigid plastic panels or flexible plastic sheeting.

Shower heads & hardware

Multiple, adjustable, and *low-flow* are the bywords for today's shower fittings. Large walk-in showers often have two or more shower heads: fixed heads at different levels, or hand units on adjustable vertical bars. Massage units often supplement the basic head or heads. The "surround" designs combine one or more fixed heads with wall-mounted auxiliary jets or adjustable multijet vertical bars. How do you control all these jets? New diverters may have three or more settings for orchestrating multiple water sources.

Safety plays a part in new designs, too. If you've ever experienced a pressure drop when someone flushes a toilet or starts the washer, you'll appreciate single-control shower fittings with pressure balancing that prevent scalding rises in temperature. Several companies also make designs that incorporate adjustable temperature limiters. You can buy quick-reacting thermostatic valves—with or without digital readouts.

Low-flow heads are required in much new construction, and many cities are making sure that less-efficient heads are replaced in remodels.

You'll probably find that low-flow retrofits splash more and are slightly noisier than standard heads. Less expensive models deliver fine droplets that won't wet your body as quickly—and might even feel a little cool by the time they get down to your knees. On/off valves are built into many low-flow heads (make sure levers are shutoffs, not just spray adjustments).

For safety and convenience, it's best to place shower controls to the front and/or side of the enclosure—*not* directly below the shower head.

ARCHITECT: CARSON BOWLER/ BOWLER & COOK ARCHITECTS

ARCHITECT: REMICK ASSOCIATES

Multiple and adjustable are the themes for shower heads and handles. Enameled hand shower (top) on adjustable mounting rod is a popular option. Temperature-control valve (middle) looks flashy, adjusts in a flash. Classic head and handles (right) suit hand-painted tile detailing. New spray bars (bottom) swivel left and right; they're part of a multihead design.

ARCHITECT: BUFF, SMITH & HENSMAN; DESIGNER: SCHLESINGER ASSOCIATES

TOILETS & BIDETS

New styling, new colors, and new efficiency are updating the tried-and-true *water closet*. In addition to standard and antique models, vitreous china toilets now come in sleek-looking European one- or two-piece designs; standard or low-profile heights; and rounded or elongated bowl shapes. Do you want classic white, shiny black, or a soft pastel? Low-flush or ultra-low-flush mechanics?

The bidet is a European standby that's steadily gaining popularity on this side of the Atlantic. It's used primarily for personal hygiene. Like toilets, bidets are made of vitreous china, in a number of styles, colors, and finishes to match toilets and other fixtures.

Toilets

As water shortages drive home the fact that water is a finite resource, the new word in toilets is *ultra-low-flush*.

Why change? Older toilets use 5 to 7 gallons or more per flush. In 1983, codes were changed to require

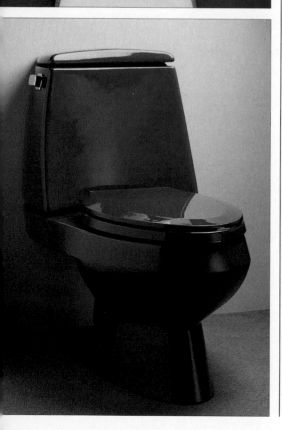

In the past, "ultra-low-flush" has sometimes meant very little flush. Pressure-assisted tank unit is one response: it uses water-compressed air to add a power boost. It's noisier than some flushing actions, but just for a moment.

New styling is transforming the trusty water closet. Trim two-piece toilet is at lower left; low-profile, one-piece model, below, has Euro-style lines and elongated bowl.

3½-gallon-per-flush toilets for new construction. But ultra-low-flush (ULF) toilets—using only 1.6 gallons or less per flush—are already replacing these in many homes. Some water districts even offer a rebate if you install one.

Some homeowners complain that ultra-low-flush toilets don't really save water in the long run because they require several flushings. One reply to this problem is the *pressure-assisted* design, which uses a strong air vacuum to power a quick, intensive flush. Pressure-assisted models are noisier than other low-flush toilets, but the disturbance is very brief.

Before installing a new toilet in an older house, check the offset—the distance between the back wall studs and the center of the drain hub (measure to the hold-down nuts). The newer models are designed for a 12-inch offset.

How about retrofits? Variable-buoyancy flappers, flap actuators that ride on the overflow tube, and dual-handle mechanisms will greatly increase the efficiency of your existing water-guzzler. They range in price from $5 to $40; some water districts will send you parts free.

Unlike water-displacement devices (jugs of water, dams, bricks), the best of the new retrofit water savers don't reduce the force of the water rushing into the bowl—the action that makes typical siphon-wash toilets work properly. With the new devices, you still have the *pressure* of the original volume, but the flap will close while several gallons still remain in the tank.

Bidets

A bidet, best installed next to the toilet, is floor-mounted and plumbed with hot and cold water. Available with wall-mount or deck-mount water controls, it comes with a spray mount or a vertical spray in the center of the bowl. Some models include rim jets to maintain bowl cleanliness. Most models also have a pop-up stopper that allows the unit to double as a foot bath or laundry basin.

Bidets, like toilets, now come in many shapes and colors. Sleek jet-black model (top) has deck-mount spray fitting. Peach-colored version (bottom) has brass handles, standpipe, and built-in spray jet; style and finish match nearby toilet.

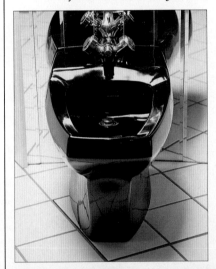

Four Flushing Actions

Washdown

Reverse trap

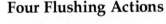

Siphon jet

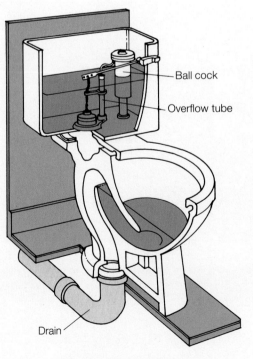

Ball cock

Overflow tube

Drain

Ultra-low-flush (ULF)

HEATING & VENTILATION

Certain elements of your bathroom's climate—steam, excess heat, early morning chill—can be annoying and unpleasant. When you remodel, consider adding an exhaust fan to freshen the air and draw out destructive moisture and a heater to warm you on cool days. Installing such climate controllers is simple, but can make a big difference. On these pages, we explore some of the heating and ventilating options.

Heating the bathroom

Nothing spoils the soothing effects of a long, hot soak or shower faster than stepping out into a cool room—or even one of average house temperature. A small auxiliary heater in the wall or ceiling may be just what you need to stay warm while toweling off. And how about a timer so you can wake up to a toasty bathing space?

Bathroom heaters warm rooms by two methods—convection (usually boosted by a small fan) and radiation. Convection heaters warm the air in a room; radiant heaters emit infrared or electromagnetic waves that warm objects and surfaces.

Electric heaters. Because electric heaters are easy to install and clean to operate, they're the most popular choice. Besides the standard wall- and ceiling-mounted units, you'll find heaters combined with exhaust fans, lights, or both. Options include thermostats, timer switches, and safety cutoffs.

Wall- or ceiling-mounted convection heaters usually have an electrically heated resistance coil and a small fan to move the heated air. Toespace heaters—recessed into a vanity below the sink—are popular.

Radiant heaters using infrared light bulbs ("heat lamps") may be

Heated towel bars keep bath linens toasty, also serve as radiators. Brass rack (left) harnesses old-fashioned hydronic heat; modern slat design (right) comes in many colors—and in both hydronic and electric versions.

ARCHITECT: REMICK ASSOCIATES

surface-mounted on the ceiling or recessed between joists.

Gas heaters. You'll find heaters available for either propane or natural gas. Though most are convection heaters, there is one radiant type—a catalytic heater. Regardless of how they heat, all gas models require a gas supply line and must be vented to the outside.

Heated towel bars. Besides gas and electricity, another heat source has reappeared on the bathroom scene: hot water. The original idea was to warm bath towels, but now these hydronic units—wall- or floor-mounted—are being billed as "radiators" as well.

Ventilating the bathroom

Even if you have good natural ventilation, an exhaust fan can exchange the air in a bathroom faster; and in bad weather, it can keep the elements out and still remove stale air. Some fans include a light or a heater or both.

It's important that your exhaust fan have adequate capacity. The Home Ventilating Institute (HVI) recommends that the fan be capable of exchanging the air at least eight times every hour. To determine the required fan capacity in cubic feet per minute (CFM) for a bathroom with an 8-foot ceiling, multiply the room's length and width in feet by 1.1. For example, if your bathroom is 6 by 9 feet, you would calculate the required fan capacity as follows:

$$6 \times 9 \times 1.1 = 59.4 \text{ CFM}$$

Rounding off, you would need fan capacity of at least 60 CFM. If your fan must exhaust through a long duct or several elbows, you'll need greater capacity to overcome the increased resistance. Follow the manufacturer's recommendations.

Most fans have a noise rating measured in sones: the lower the number, the quieter the fan.

Most modern vents and heaters are trim, discreet, built-ins. Ceiling fan (top) blends with white field tiles, draws heat and moisture from steam shower. Electric toespace heater (bottom), centered below sink area, emits welcome warmth on chilly mornings.

Three Paths for a Vent Duct

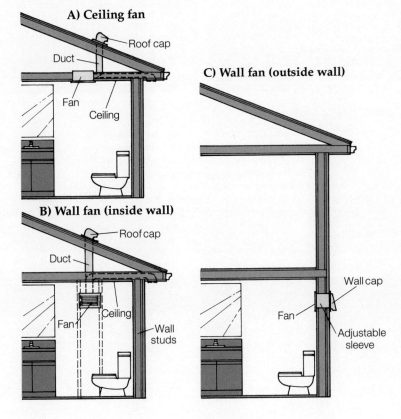

A) Ceiling fan
Roof cap
Duct
Fan
Ceiling

B) Wall fan (inside wall)
Roof cap
Duct
Fan
Ceiling
Wall studs

C) Wall fan (outside wall)
Wall cap
Fan
Adjustable sleeve

ARCHITECT: REMICK ASSOCIATES

FLOORING

Two primary requirements for a bathroom floor are moisture resistance and durability. Resilient tiles and sheets, ceramic tile, and properly sealed masonry or hardwood are all good candidates. Resilient flooring is the simplest (and usually the least expensive) to install; the others are trickier. For a touch of comfort, don't rule out carpeting, especially newer stain resistant, industrial versions.

Planning checkpoints

Confused by the array of flooring types available? For help, study the guide below. Also, it's a good idea to visit flooring suppliers and home improvement centers; most dealers are happy to provide samples.

For safety's sake, a bathroom floor must be slip resistant, especially in wet areas. Tiles, either ceramic or resilient, are safest in mat-finish

---

COMPARING FLOORING

Resilient

Advantages. Generally made from solid vinyl or polyurethane, resilients are flexible, moisture and stain resistant, easy to install, and simple to maintain. Another advantage is the seemingly endless variety of colors, textures, patterns, and styles available. Tiles can be mixed to form custom patterns or provide color accents.

Sheets run up to 12 feet wide, eliminating the need for seaming in many bathrooms; tiles are generally 12 inches square. Vinyl and rubber are comfortable to walk on. A polyurethane finish eliminates the need for waxing.

Disadvantages. Resilients are relatively soft, making them vulnerable to dents and tears; often, though, such damage can be repaired. Tiles may collect moisture between seams if improperly installed. Some vinyl still comes with a photographically applied pattern, but most is inlaid; the latter is more expensive, but wears much better.

Cost. Prices (uninstalled) range from about $1.50 a square foot for the least expensive tile to nearly $15. Sheet vinyls range from about 35 cents to $5.50. Expect to pay a premium for custom tiles and for imported products.

Ceramic tile

Advantages. Made from hard-fired slabs of clay, ceramic tile is available in dozens of patterns, colors, shapes, and finishes. Its durability, easy upkeep, and attractiveness are definite advantages.

Tiles are usually classified as *quarry tile,* commonly unglazed (unfinished) red-clay tiles that are rough and water resistant; *pavers,* rugged unglazed tiles in earth-tone shades; and *glazed tile,* available in glossy, mat, or textured finishes and in many colors.

Tile sizes run a gamut of widths, lengths, and thicknesses: by mixing sizes and colors, creative tile workers can fashion a wide range of border treatments and field accents.

Disadvantages. Tile can be cold, noisy, and, if glazed, slippery underfoot. If not properly grouted, tiles can leak moisture; some tiles will stain unless properly sealed. Grout spaces can be tough to keep clean.

Cost. Tile can cost from about $1 per square foot to nearly $40, uninstalled. Those with three-dimensional patterns and multicolored glazes can easily cost double. Purer clays fired at higher temperatures generally make costlier but better-wearing tiles.

versions. If you're installing custom ceramic tile, you can add sand to the glaze. Smaller tiles, with their extra grout spaces, offer extra texture (and traction). A rubberized mat or throw rug (if it will stay put) can provide firm footing—and a warm landing zone—near the tub or shower.

Don't be afraid to mix and match flooring materials. Today's layouts often use different materials in wet and dry areas. Cozy carpeting is showing up frequently in dressing areas, grooming centers, and even exercise rooms. If you're on a budget, save the polished marble or fine ceramic tile for a focal point, such as around a pedestal tub or walk-in shower.

What about subflooring?

Don't make any final flooring decision until you know the kind and condition of the subfloor your new flooring will cover.

With proper preparation, a concrete slab can serve as a base for almost any type of flooring. Other subfloors are more flexible and not suitable for rigid materials such as masonry and ceramic tile unless they are built up with extra underlayment or floor framing. Too many layers underneath can make the bathroom floor awkwardly higher than surrounding rooms. Be sure to check with a building professional or a flooring dealer for specifics.

COMPARING FLOORING

Stone

Advantages. Natural stone (such as slate, flagstone, marble, granite, and limestone) has been used as flooring for centuries. Today, its use is even more practical, thanks to the development of sealers and finishes. Easy to maintain, masonry flooring is also virtually indestructible. Stone can be used in its natural shape or cut into rectangular blocks or more formal tiles. Generally, pieces are butted tightly together; irregular flagstone requires grouted joints.

Disadvantages. The cost of most masonry flooring is high. Moreover, the weight of the materials requires a very strong, well-supported subfloor. Some stone—marble in particular—is cold and slippery underfoot. Careful sealing is a must; certain stones, such as limestone or granite, absorb stains and dirt readily.

Cost. From $3 per square foot for slate to $30 and over for granite.

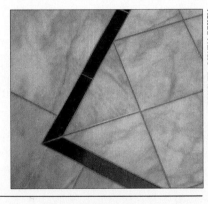

DESIGNER: OSBURN DESIGN

ARCHITECT: PETER C. RODI/DESIGNBANK

Hardwood

Advantages. A classic hardwood floor creates a warm decor, feels good underfoot and can be refinished. Oak is most common; maple, birch, and beech are also available.

The three basic types are narrow strips in random lengths; planks in various widths and random lengths; and wood tiles, laid in blocks or squares. "Floating" floor systems have several veneered strips atop each backing board. Wood flooring may be factory-prefinished or unfinished, to be sanded and finished in place.

Disdavantages. Moisture damage and inadequate floor substructure are two bugaboos. Maintenance is another issue; some surfaces can be mopped, some cannot. Bleaching and some staining processes may wear unevenly and are difficult to repair.

Cost. From $7.50 to $13 per square foot, installed, depending on type, quality, and finish. Floating systems are generally most expensive.

Carpeting

Advantages. Carpeting cushions feet, provides firm traction, and helps deaden sound. It's especially useful to define areas in multiuse layouts or master suites. New tightly woven commercial products are making carpeting a more practical option.

Disadvantages. Generally, the more elaborate the material and weave, the greater the problems from moisture absorption, staining, and mildew. Carpeting used in bathrooms should be short-pile and unsculptured. Woven or loop-pile wool should be confined to dressing areas. Nylon and other synthetic carpets are a better choice for splash zones; these are washable and hold up well in moist conditions.

Cost. Like resilient flooring, carpeting is available in an array of styles and materials with prices that vary widely. Synthetics average around $30 per yard; fine natural fibers may easily top $100.

DESIGNER: DIANE JOHNSON DESIGN

WALLS & CEILINGS

Bathroom wall and ceiling treatments must be able to withstand moisture, heat, and high usage. These surfaces also go a long way toward defining the overall impact of your bath. Below, we survey the options.

Wall coverings

In addition to the shower and tub-surround areas, your bathroom will probably include a good bit of wall space. Here are nine popular treatments.

Paint. Of course, everybody thinks of paint first. But what's best for the bathroom? Your basic choices are latex and alkyd paint.

Latex is easy to work with, and best of all, you can clean up wet paint with soap and water. Alkyd paint (often called oil-base paint) provides high gloss and will hang on a little harder than latex; however, alkyds are harder to apply and require cleanup with mineral spirits.

In general, high resin content is the mark of durable, abrasion-resistant, flexible paint—the kind you need in a bathroom. Usually, the higher the resin content, the higher the gloss; so look for products labeled gloss or semigloss if you want a tough, washable finish.

An excellent choice for bathroom cabinets and woodwork is interior/exterior, quick-drying alkyd enamel;

Even bathroom walls are sporting a new look. On the facing page, decorative sponged paint on wall and vanity complements random slate backsplash with custom grout. At right, colored joint compound was knife-applied over lighter base tint; top glaze accents both.

it has a brilliant, tilelike finish that's extremely durable.

Faux finishing. Faux (literally, *false*) painting finishes produce the appearance of other patterns or textures.

In one version, many closely related pastels are built up in subtle layers with brush strokes, by stippling, or with a sponge. Other faux finishes are bolder—including layers of textured paint and/or contrasting colors to mimic anything from traditional wallpaper to modern art.

Ceramic tile. Tough, water-resistant tile is always a good choice for a bathroom, and the range of colors, textures, shapes, and sizes opens up many creative possibilities.

Wall tiles are typically glazed, and offer great variety in color and design. Generally lighter than floor tiles, their relatively light weight is a plus for vertical installation. Standard sizes range from 3-inch squares to 4¼- by 8½-inch rectangles; thickness varies from ¼ to ⅜ inch.

Ceramic mosaic is one of the most colorful and versatile materials in the tile family. Tiles sold under this name are generally small—2 by 2 inches or less. They come in sheets, mounted on thread mesh or paper backing or joined with silicone rub-

DESIGNER: OSBURN DESIGN

ARCHITECT: REMICK ASSOCIATES

DESIGNER: CHARLOTTE BOYLE INTERIORS; ARCHITECT: J. ALLEN SAYLES

ber. You can install mosaics on curved surfaces, too. Once they're in place, you grout these sheets like any other wall tiles.

Stone. Marble, slate, limestone, and granite, whether as 8- or 12-inch tiles or wider sheets, can perform a similar role to ceramic tile. Though these natural materials can be costly, there's no reason to break the bank: a small accent can go a long way. Try a dash of stone along the tub pedestal, along the backsplash, around the shower, or as wainscoting on one prominent wall.

Most stone, especially marble, should be thoroughly sealed for wall use; untreated, it can be stained or eaten away by acids in cleaning supplies or even household water.

Glass block. If you're looking for some ambient daylight but don't want to lose your privacy, consider another old-timer—glass block. It provides a soft, filtered light that complements many bath designs.

You can buy 3- or 4-inch-thick square blocks in many sizes; rectangular blocks are available in a more limited selection. Textures range from smooth to wavy, rippled, bubbly, or crosshatched. To locate glass block, look in the yellow pages under Glass—Block Structural, Etc. You may be able to special-order blocks through a regular glass dealer.

Wallpaper. A wallpaper for the bathroom should be scrubbable, durable, and stain resistant. Solid vinyl wallpapers, which come in a wide variety of colors and textures, fill the bill. New patterns, including some that replicate other surfaces (such as linen), are generally subtle; wallpaper borders add visual punch to ceiling lines and openings. Good ventilation is crucial to keep wallpaper from loosening.

Glass blocks are a natural for the bath. At upper left, they line walls behind walk-in shower and tub, letting in light and color while maintaining privacy. Dark green square tiles and trim (left) create a classic accent to white tile wainscoting.

Fabric. Although upholstered walls probably don't leap to mind, consider them for powder rooms where there's no shower or tub. Upholstered walls can add a dash of style, and also a measure of soundproofing.

Plaster. The textured, uneven, and slightly rounded edges of plaster give a bathroom a custom, informal look; plaster is especially popular for Southwest-theme designs. The only drawback: if the surface is too irregular, it's hard to keep clean.

Wood. Tongue-and-groove wood paneling—natural, stained, bleached, or painted—provides a charming accent to country schemes. Wainscoting is most popular, separated from wallpaper or paint above by the traditional chair rail.

Moldings are back in vogue. Specialty shops are likely to have a wide selection and will often custom-match an old favorite to order.

Ceiling treatments

Don't worry—you needn't be stuck with that old acoustic ceiling. Here's a brief survey of the alternatives.

Open it up. If your one-story house has an attic or crawl space above, you may be able to remove ceiling joists—or add more widely spaced beams—and forgo the ceiling material. Track lights and hanging pendants are useful accompaniments. You'll need to finish off the underside of the roof decking, either with tongue-and-groove wood planks or with drywall and paint. And, of course, this would be the perfect time to add a skylight.

Add hollow beams. Certain home styles—for example, French country—incorporate patterned beams and enclosed ceiling bays (usually painted wallboard). The hollow beams are built up from 2-by lumber and molding, and provide a bonus: the inner raceways are efficient spots to hide electrical and plumbing lines or heating ducts.

Wallpaper, whether used overall, above wainscoting, or simply for an ornate border, is showing new flair. The powder room above wears a hand-painted, hand-embossed pattern. Don't rule out upholstery (right): its benefits include elegant color, soft texture, and good soundproofing.

DESIGNER: LEGALLET-TRINKNER DESIGN ASSOCIATES
UPHOLSTERY: DOUGLAS GRIGGS/HANG UPS

Lower it. You can remedy a bumpy or worn-out surface, glaring ceiling panels, or a too-tall space in one of two ways. If there is no framework, install horizontal ceiling joists, then apply a wallboard ceiling and finish it as you wish. Over an existing ceiling, you can nail 1-by furring strips, then add wallboard.

Size up the soffits. An open soffit between wall cabinets and ceiling can house uplighting to "lift" a ceiling. Or enclose the area with wallboard or molded plaster, perhaps extending the soffits past the cabinet fronts and adding recessed downlights (see pages 89–91).

Remember that wood crown or cove moldings can help dress up any ceiling soffit.

ARCHITECT: TED T. TANAKA

Windows & skylights

After years of timidly testing the balance between the need for privacy and the desire for a view, bathrooms are now taking advantage, in earnest, of available light and sights.

Need to add light? Here are four basic strategies for lightening up without baring all:

■ *Rise above your neighbors.* Putting the bath near the top of your house can give you both panorama and privacy.

■ *Annex a view and enclose it.* Convert a portion of your landscape to create a low-maintenance view garden. Deep overhangs can cut direct glare; an encircling wall can ensure privacy.

■ *Install an openable skylight.* Roof windows let in light and make a space feel roomier. When open, skylights exhaust stale air and moisture.

■ *Maximize light and edit the view.* You can combine glass in different forms (panels, blocks) and finishes (clear, translucent) to bring in more light and view while still protecting personal privacy. Generally, transparent materials are suitable above chin height of the tallest occupant. But check the heights and locations of neighbors' windows.

What units are out there? Windows, available in many styles, may be wood, aluminum, vinyl, or steel. Vinyl- or aluminum-clad wood windows and all-vinyl windows require little maintenance.

Though you can have a skylight custom-made, there is also a wide range of prefabricated units. Some can be opened, by motor or by hand—a big plus for ventilation.

If there's space between the ceiling and roof, you'll need a light shaft to direct light to the room below. It may be straight, angled, or splayed.

Both windows and skylights can bring new life to landlocked interiors. In this compact, marble-dressed bath, a custom skylight and light shaft yield sunshine—and a welcome feeling of space.

LIGHT FIXTURES

Designers separate lighting into three categories: task, ambient, and accent. Task lighting illuminates a particular area where a visual activity—such as shaving or applying makeup—takes place. Ambient (or general) lighting fills in the undefined areas of a room with a soft level of light—enough, say, for a relaxing soak in a whirlpool tub. Accent lighting, which is primarily decorative, is used to highlight architectural features, to set a mood, or to provide drama.

Which fixtures are best?

Generally speaking, *small* and *discreet* are themes for bathroom lighting; consequently, recessed downlights are very popular. Fitted with the right baffle or shield, these fixtures alone can handle ambient, task, and accent needs.

In a larger bathroom, a separate fixture to light the shower or bath area—or any other distinct part in a compartmentalized design—and perhaps one for reading may be appreciated. Shower fixtures should be waterproof units with neoprene seals.

Fixtures around a makeup or shaving mirror should spread light over a person's face rather than onto the mirror surface. To avoid heavy shadows, it's best to place mirror lights at the sides, rather than only

Low-voltage downlights, filtered sunlight, and wall mirrors work their magic in this small tub area. The mirrors reflect the light many times over, but there's no glare: slot apertures help focus each MR-16 bulb.

overhead. Wall sconces flanking the mirror not only provide light, but offer an opportunity for a stylish design statement.

And just for fun, why not consider decorative uplights in a soffit, or strip lights in a toespace area? These low-key accents help provide a wash of ambient light and can also serve as safe, pleasant night lights.

Dimmers (also called rheostats) enable you to set a fixture or group of fixtures at any level of illumination from a soft glow to radiant brightness. They also save energy.

Light bulbs & tubes

Light sources can be grouped in general categories according to the way they produce light.

Incandescent light. This light, the kind used most frequently in our homes, is produced by a tungsten thread that burns slowly inside a

LIGHTING DESIGNER: DONALD MAXCY

Well-chosen lighting can help jazz up a powder room. In the one above, task and ambient lighting emanate from dimmer-controlled halogen wall fixtures; mirrors bounce light around, stretch space, and add fun, too. The diamond-patterned marble border is accented by hidden low-voltage strip lights, detailed at right.

LIGHT
FIXTURES

glass bulb. A-bulbs are the old stand-bys; R and PAR bulbs produce a more controlled beam; silvered-bowl types diffuse light. A number of decorative bulbs are also available.

Low-voltage incandescent lighting is especially useful for accent lighting. Operating on 12 or 24 volts, these lights require transformers (which are often built into the fixtures) to step down the voltage from standard 120-volt household circuits.

Low-voltage fixtures are relatively expensive to buy; but in general, low-voltage lighting can be energy- and cost-efficient if carefully planned.

Fluorescent light. Fluorescent tubes are unrivaled for energy efficiency; they also last far longer than incandescent bulbs. In some energy-conscious areas, general lighting for new bathrooms *must* be fluorescent.

Older fluorescent tubes have been criticized for noise, flicker, and poor color rendition. Electronic ballasts and better fixture shielding against glare have remedied the first two problems; as for the last one, manufacturers have developed fluorescents in a wide spectrum of colors, from very warm (about 2,700 degrees K) to very cool (about 6,300 degrees K).

Quartz halogen. These bright, white newcomers are excellent for task lighting, pinpoint accenting, and other dramatic accents. Halogen is usually low-voltage but may use standard line current. The popular MR-16 bulb creates the tightest beam; for a longer reach and wider coverage, choose a PAR bulb. There's an abundance of smaller bulb shapes and sizes to fit pendants and under-cabinet strip lights.

Halogen has two disadvantages: its high initial cost and its very high heat. Be sure to shop carefully. Some fixtures on the market are not UL-approved.

COMPARING LIGHT BULBS & TUBES

INCANDESCENT

A-bulb

Description. Familiar pear shape; frosted or clear.
Uses. Everyday household use.

T—Tubular

Description. Tube-shaped, from 5" long. Frosted or clear.
Uses. Appliances, cabinets, decorative fixtures.

R—Reflector

Description. White or silvered coating directs light out end of funnel-shaped bulb.
Uses. In directional fixtures; focuses light where needed.

PAR—Parabolic aluminized reflector

Description. Similar to auto headlamp; special shape and coating project light and control beam.
Uses. In recessed downlights and track fixtures.

Silvered bowl

Description. A-bulb, with silvered cap to cut glare and produce indirect light.
Uses. In track fixtures and pendants.

Low-voltage strip lights

Description. Like Christmas tree lights; in strips or tracks, or encased in flexible, waterproof plastic.
Uses. Task lighting and decoration.

FLUORESCENT

Tube

Description. Tube-shaped, 5" to 96" long. Needs special fixture and ballast.
Uses. Shadowless work light; also indirect lighting.

PL—Compact tube

Description. U-shaped with base; 5¼" to 7½" long.
Uses. In recessed downlights; some PL tubes include ballasts to replace A-bulbs.

QUARTZ HALOGEN

High-intensity

Description. Small, clear bulb with consistently high light output; used in halogen fixtures.
Uses. In specialized task lamps, torchères, and pendants.

Low-voltage MR-16 (mini-reflector)

Description. Tiny (2"-diameter) projector bulb; gives small circle of light from a distance.
Uses. In low-voltage track fixtures, mono-spots, and recessed downlights.

Low-voltage PAR

Description. Similar to auto headlamp, tiny filament, shape, and coating give precise direction.
Uses. To project a small spot of light a long distance.

FINISHING TOUCHES

In bathroom design as in life, it's sometimes the little things that count. Here's a quick look at some of the amenities that can furnish delightful finishing touches.

Accessory lines are more complete than ever; some towel bars, hooks, and tissue holders even correspond with faucet handles on sinks, tubs, and showers. Additional matchables may include cabinet pulls, switch plates, mirrors, light fixtures, and wall tiles. And how about a pedestal sink or bathtub that's part of the same collection?

Other popular amenities include adjustable makeup mirrors (typically 3x to 5x), with or without optical glass and internal illumination; shaving mirrors for the shower; heated towel-bar warmers or "radiators" (discussed on pages 80–81); and home entertainment components (TVs, ceiling-mounted speakers, control panels wired to compact disk players and AM/FM tuners).

Hardware helps give a plain bathroom a sense of style. Optical make-up mirror (near right) comes in tabletop and wall-mount versions; pivoting towel rod (far right) accents scalloped pedestal sink. Photo below right shows one of many matching sets available. Don't forget to choose cabinet pulls or knobs (below).

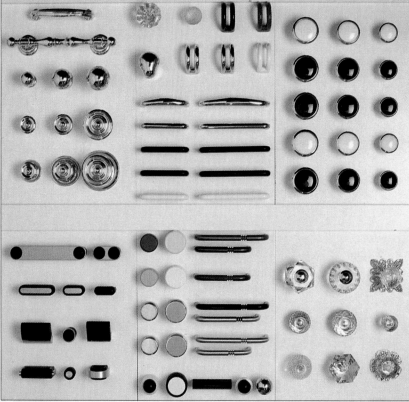

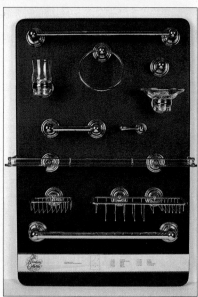

In addition to fine design and craftsmanship, bathroom on facing page gains visual coherence from an integrated product line. Coordinated components extend from fixtures—tub, toilet, and sink—to wall lights, mirror, shelves, and wall tiles.

INFORMATION SOURCES

When you're transforming an old bathroom into one that's innovative and efficient, you'll find a wealth of ideas and information in brochures put out by the various manufacturers listed on these pages. They can also tell you about local outlets and distributors for their products. The addresses and phone numbers in this list are accurate as of press time.

The yellow pages of your telephone directory and the National Kitchen & Bath Association (124 Main Street, Hackettstown, NJ 07840) can help you locate bathroom showrooms, cabinetmakers, designers, architects, and other sources near you.

BARRIER-FREE HARDWARE

Hewi, Inc.
2851 Old Tree Drive
Lancaster, PA 17603
717-293-1313

Normbau, Inc.
Box 930
Mt. Washington, KY 40047
800-356-2920

CABINETS

Allmilmö Corp.
70 Clinton Road
Fairfield, NJ 07004
201-227-2502

Crystal Cabinet Works, Inc.
1100 Crystal Drive
Princeton, MN 55371
612-389-4187

Dura Supreme, Inc.
Box K
Howard Lake, MN 55349
612-543-3872

Kraftmaid Cabinetry, Inc.
16052 Industrial Parkway
Middlefield, OH 44062
216-632-5333

Merillat Industries, Inc.
5353 W. US 223
Adrian, MI 49221
517-263-0771

Poggenpohl US, Inc.
5905 Johns Road
Tampa, FL 33634
813-882-9292

Quaker Maid
WCI, Inc.
Route 61
Leesport, PA 19533
215-926-3011

Robern, Inc.
1648 Winchester Road
Bensalem, PA 19020
215-245-6550

Sears Roebuck & Company
Sears Tower
Department 610
Chicago, IL 60684
312-875-2500

SieMatic Corp.
886 Town Center Drive
Langhorn, PA 19047
215-750-1928

Smallbone, Inc.
150 E. 58th Street
New York, NY 10155
212-935-3222

Snaidero West, Inc.
Pacific Design Center
8687 Melrose Avenue B487
Los Angeles, CA 90069
213-854-0222

Wm Ohs Cabinets
5095 Peoria Street
Denver, CO 80239
303-371-6550

Wood-Mode Inc.
Wood Metal Industries
One Second Street
Kreamer, PA 17833
717-374-2711

COUNTERTOPS

American Olean Tile Co., Inc.
Box 271
Lansdale, PA 19446
215-855-1111

Avonite, Inc.
1945 Highway 304S
Belen, NM 87002
800-428-6648

Color Tile, Inc.
Box 2475
Fort Worth, TX 76113
817-870-9400

Corian Building Products
E. I. DuPont de Nemours & Co.
1007 Market Street
Wilmington, DE 19898
800-426-7426

Dal-Tile Corp.
7834 Hawn Freeway
Dallas, TX 75217
214-398-1411

Formica Corp.
One Stanford Road
Box 338
Piscataway, NJ 08854-55
908-469-1555

Nevamar Corp.
8339 Telegraph Road
Odenton, MD 21113
301-551-5000

Summitville Tiles, Inc.
Box 73
Summitville, OH 43962
216-223-1511

Wilsonart
Ralph Wilson Plastics Co.
600 General Bruce Drive
Temple, TX 76501
800-433-3222
800-792-6000 (Texas)

FITTINGS & HARDWARE

American Standard, Inc.
U.S. Plumbing Products
Box 6820
Piscataway, NJ 08855
908-980-3000

Artistic Brass
4100 Ardmore Avenue
South Gate, CA 90280
213-564-1100

The Chicago Faucet Co.
2100 S. Nuclear Drive
Des Plaines, IL 60018
312-694-4400

Culligan International Co.
One Culligan Parkway
Northbrook, IL 60062
708-205-6000

Delta Faucet Co.
55 E. 111th Street
Box 40980
Indianapolis, IN 46280
317-848-1812

Everpure, Inc.
660 N. Blackhawk Drive
Westmont, IL 60559
708-654-4000

Grohe America, Inc.
900 Lively Boulevard
Wood Dale, IL 60191
708-350-2600

Hansa America
931 W. 19th Street
Chicago, IL 60608
312-733-0025

Hansgrohe Inc.
2840 Research Park Drive
Suite 100
Soquel, Ca 95073
408-479-0515

Harrington Brass Works,
Ltd., Inc.
166 Coolidge Avenue
Englewood, NJ 07631
201-871-6011

Kallista, Inc.
1355 Market Street, #105
San Francisco, CA 94103
415-895-6400

Kohler Co.
444 Highland Drive
Kohler, WI 53044
800-456-4537, ext. 263

KWC Faucets
Western States Manufac-
turing Corp.
1559 Sunland Lane
Costa Mesa, CA 92626
714-557-1933

Möen, Inc.
377 Woodland Avenue
Elyria, OH 44036
800-347-6636

Paul Associates
155 E. 55th Street
New York, NY 10022
212-755-1313

Villeroy & Boch USA, Inc.
Box 103
Pine Brook, NJ 07058
201-575-0550

FIXTURES & APPLIANCES

American Standard, Inc.
U.S. Plumbing Products
Box 6820
Piscataway, NJ 08855
908-980-3000

Bates & Bates
3699 Industry Avenue
Lakewood, CA 90712
800-726-7680

Eljer Industries
Box 869037
Plano, TX 75086-9037
800-753-5537

Jacuzzi Whirlpool Bath
Drawer J
Walnut Creek, CA 94596
800-678-6889

Kohler Co.
444 Highland Drive
Kohler, WI 53044
800-456-4537, ext. 263

Luwa Corp.
Box 16348
Charlotte, NC 28297
704-394-8341

Mansfield-Norris Plumbing
Fixtures
700 Fairway Drive
Walnut, CA 91788
818-965-3394

Miele Appliances, Inc.
22D Worlds Fair Drive
Somerset, NJ 08873
908-560-0899

Mr. Steam
43-20 34th Street
Long Island City, NY 11101
800-767-8326

Porcher, Inc.
650 Maple Avenue
Torrance, CA 90503
213-212-6112

Sterling Plumbing Group,
Inc.
1375 Remington Road
Schaumburg, IL 60173
708-843-5400

Villeroy & Boch USA, Inc.
Box 103
Pine Brook, NJ 07058
201-575-0550

FLOORING

American Olean Tile Co.,
Inc.
Box 271
Lansdale, PA 19446-0271
215-855-1111

Armstrong World
Industries, Inc.
Box 3001
Lancaster, PA 17604
800-233-3823

Bruce Hardwood Floors
Box 660100
Dallas, TX 75266-0100
214-931-3000

Color Tile, Inc.
Box 2475
Fort Worth, TX 76113
817-870-9400

Congoleum Corp.
861 Sloan Avenue
Trenton, NJ 08619
609-584-3000

Dal-Tile Corp.
7834 Hawn Freeway
Dallas, TX 75217
214-398-1411

Mannington Mills, Inc.
Box 30
Salem, NJ 08079
609-935-3000

Summitville Tiles, Inc.
Box 73
Summitville, OH 43962
216-223-1511

The Tileshop
1005 Harrison Street
Berkeley, CA 94710
510-525-4312

HEATING & VENTILATION

Broan Mfg. Co., Inc.
Box 140
Hartford, WI 53027
414-673-4340

Casablanca Fan Co.
Box 424
City of Industry, CA 91747
818-369-6441

Hunter Fan Co.
2500 Frisco Avenue
Memphis, TN 38114
901-743-1360

Myson, Inc.
Box 7789
Fredricksburg, VA 22404
703-371-4331

NuTone, Inc.
Madison & Red Bank roads
Cincinnati, OH 45227
513-527-5100

Runtal North America, Inc.
187 Neck Road
Ward Hill, MA 01835
800-526-2621

LIGHT FIXTURES

Casablanca Fan Co.
Box 424
City of Industry, CA 91747
818-369-6441

Halo Lighting
Cooper Lighting
6842 Walker Street
La Palma, CA 90623
714-522-7171

Hunter Fan Co.
2500 Frisco Avenue
Memphis, TN 38114
901-743-1360

Lightolier/Genlyte, Inc.
100 Lighting Way
Secaucus, NJ 07096-1508
201-864-3000

Progress Lighting
G Street & Erie Avenue
Philadelphia, PA 19134
215-289-1200

STORAGE PRODUCTS

Closet Maid
Clairson International
720 SW 17th Street
Ocala, FL 32674
904-351-6100

Elfa
Eurica Marketing, Inc.
1760 East Wilshire Avenue
Santa Ana, CA 92705
714-285-1000

Iron-A-Way, Inc.
220 W. Jackson
Morton, IL 61550
309-266-7232

Rev-a-Shelf, Inc.
Box 99585
Jeffersontown, KY 40299
800-626-1126
502-499-5835

Rubbermaid Inc.
1147 Akron Road
Wooster, OH 44691
216-264-6464

NuTone, Inc.
Madison & Red Bank roads
Cincinnati, OH 45227
513-527-5100

INDEX